EASY PROGRESSIVE
GUITAR PIE

Arranged by Mark Phillips

ISBN 978-1-4950-5873-8

HAL•LEONARD®
CORPORATION

7777 W. BLUEMOUND RD. P.O. BOX 13819 MILWAUKEE, WI 53213

Visit Hal Leonard Online at
www.halleonard.com

This Land Is Your Land

Words and Music by Woody Guthrie

Blowin' in the Wind

Words and Music by Bob Dylan

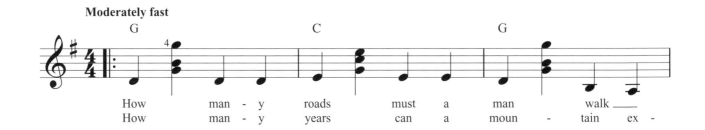

Moderately fast

How man - y roads must a man walk ___
How man - y years can a moun - tain ex -

down be - fore you call him a
ist be - fore it is washed to the

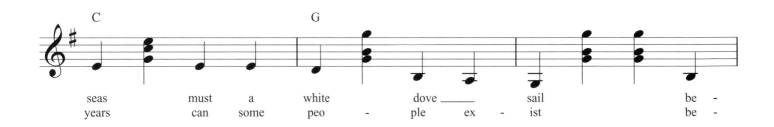

man? How man - y
sea? How man - y

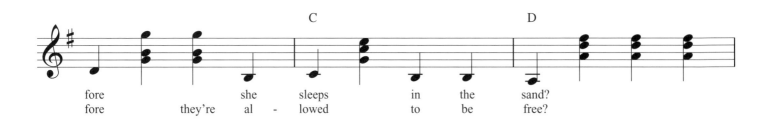

seas must a white dove ___ sail be -
years can some peo - ple ex - ist be -

fore she sleeps in the sand?
fore they're al - lowed to be free?

G   C

How man - y times must the
How man - y times can a

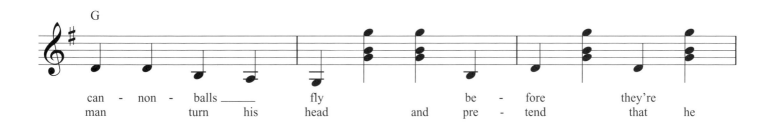

G

can - non - balls _____ fly be - fore they're
man turn his head and pre - tend that he

C   G

for - ev - er banned?
just does - n't see?

The

C   D   G

an - swer, my friend, is blow - in' in the

C   D

wind. The an - swer is blow - in' in the

1.   2.

G

wind.

Daydream Believer

Words and Music by John Stewart

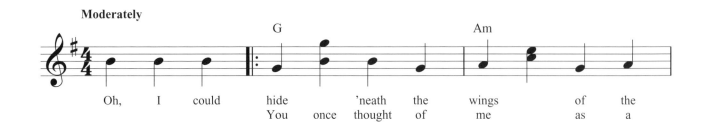

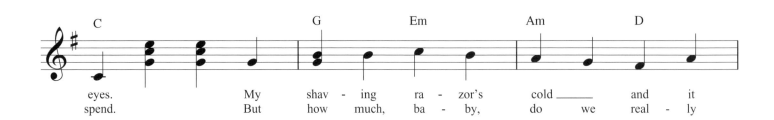

stings.
need?

Cheer up, sleep - y

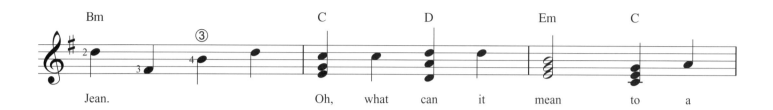

Jean.

Oh, what can it mean to a

day - dream be - liev - er and a home - com - ing

queen?

Unchained Melody

Lyric by Hy Zaret
Music by Alex North

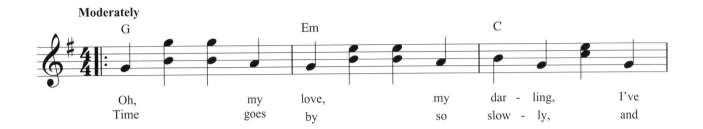

Oh, my love, my dar - ling, I've
Time goes by so slow - ly, and

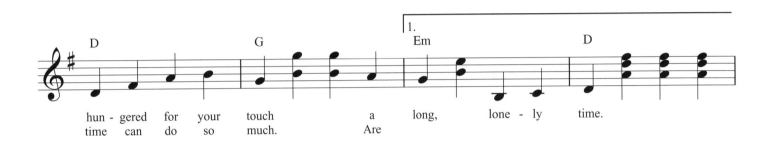

hun - gered for your touch a long, lone - ly time.
time can do so much. Are

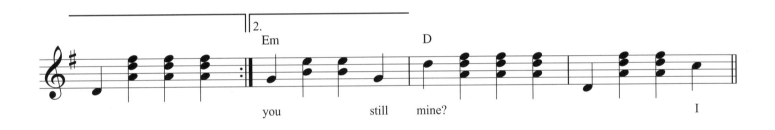

you still mine? I

need your love, I need your love. God

speed your love to me.

Lone - ly riv - ers flow to the sea, to the
Lone - ly riv - ers sigh, "Wait for me, wait for

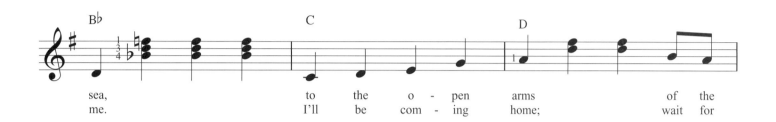

sea, to the o - pen arms of the
me. I'll be com - ing home; wait for

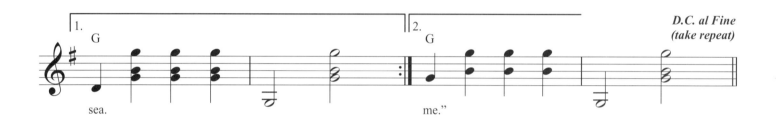

D.C. al Fine
(take repeat)

sea. me."

Mr. Tambourine Man

Words and Music by Bob Dylan

Moderately fast

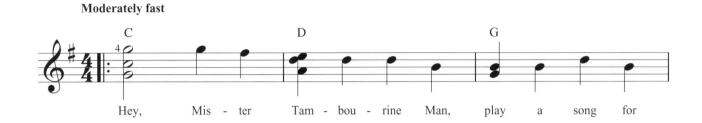

Hey, Mis - ter Tam - bou - rine Man, play a song for

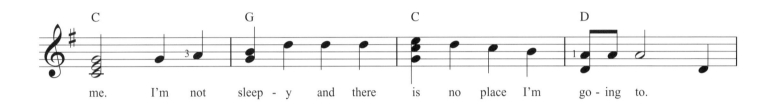

me. I'm not sleep - y and there is no place I'm go - ing to.

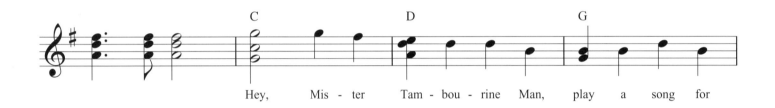

Hey, Mis - ter Tam - bou - rine Man, play a song for

me. In the jin - gle jan - gle morn - ing I'll come fol - low - ing

Fine

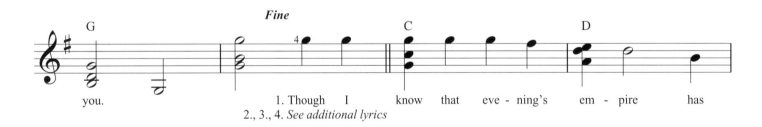

you.   1. Though I know that eve - ning's em - pire has

2., 3., 4. *See additional lyrics*

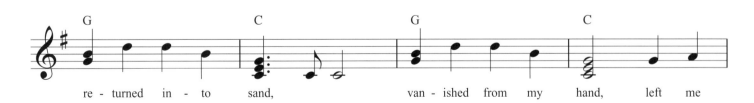

re - turned in - to sand, van - ished from my hand, left me

blind - ly here to stand but still not sleep - ing, my

wea - ri - ness a - maz - es me. I'm brand - ed on my feet. I

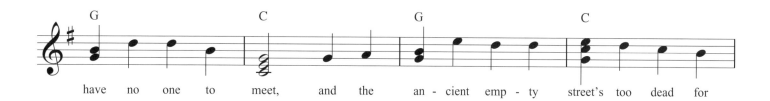

have no one to meet, and the an - cient emp - ty street's too dead for

1., 2., 3.   4.   *D.C. al Fine*

dream - ing.

Additional Lyrics

2. Take me on a trip upon your magic swirlin' ship.
   My senses have been stripped; my hands can't feel to grip.
   My toes too numb to step.
   Wait only for my boot heels to be wanderin'.
   I'm ready to go anywhere; I'm ready for to fade
   Into my own parade; cast your dancing spell my way.
   I promise to go under it.

3. Though you might hear laughin', spinnin', swingin' madly across the sun,
   It's not aimed at anyone; it's just escapin' on the run,
   And but for the sky there are no fences facin'.
   And if you hear vague traces of skippin' reels of rhyme
   To your tambourine in time, it's just a ragged clown behind.
   I wouldn't pay it any mind.
   It's just a shadow you're seein' that he's chasing.

4. Then take me disappearin' through the smoke rings of my mind,
   Down the foggy ruins of time, far past the frozen leaves,
   The haunted, frightened trees, out to the windy beach,
   Far from the twisted reach of crazy sorrow.
   Yes, to dance beneath the diamond sky with one hand waving free,
   Silhouetted by the sea, circled by the circus sands,
   With all memory and fate driven deep beneath the waves.
   Let me forget about today until tomorrow.

Leaving on a Jet Plane

Words and Music by John Denver

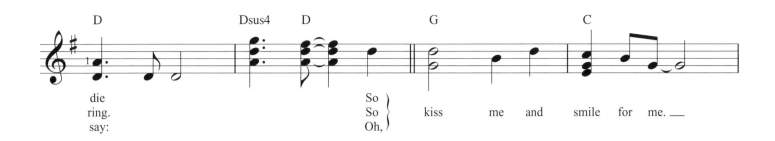

die
ring.   So
say: So } kiss   me   and   smile   for   me. __
                                   Oh,

Tell   me   that __   you'll   wait   for   me. __   Hold   me   like __   you'll

nev - er   let   me   go.   'Cause   I'm

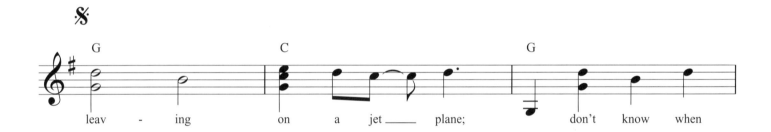

leav - ing   on   a   jet __   plane;   don't   know   when

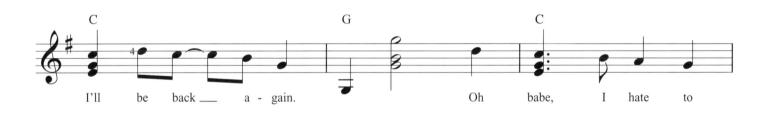

I'll   be   back __   a - gain.   Oh   babe,   I   hate   to

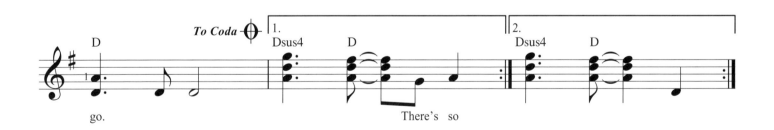

go.   There's   so

3.

'Cause   I'm

The Sound of Silence

Words and Music by Paul Simon

1. Hel - lo, dark-ness, my old friend,

2.-5. See additional lyrics

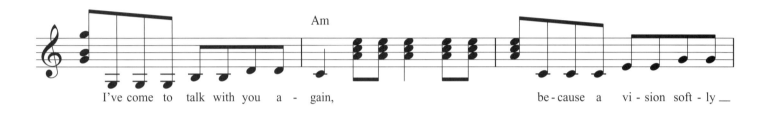

I've come to talk with you a - gain, be - cause a vi - sion soft - ly __

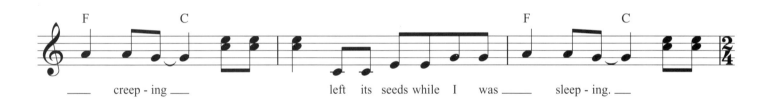

__ creep - ing __ left its seeds while I was __ sleep - ing. __

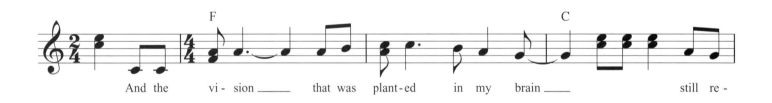

And the vi - sion __ that was plant-ed in my brain __ still re -

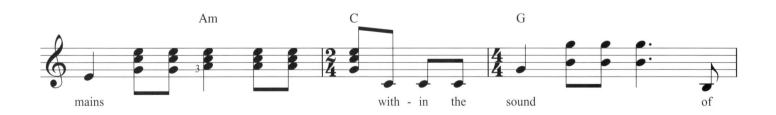

mains with - in the sound of

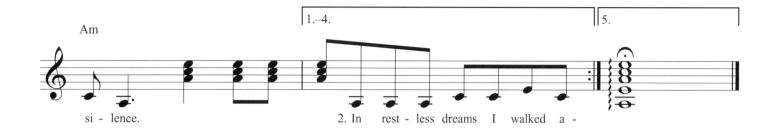

si - lence.   2. In   rest - less dreams   I   walked a -

Additional Lyrics

2. In restless dreams I walked alone,
   Narrow streets of cobblestone.
   'Neath the halo of a streetlamp,
   I turned my collar to the cold and damp,
   When my eyes were stabbed by the flash of a neon light
   That split the night and touched the sound of silence.

3. And in the naked light I saw
   Ten thousand people, maybe more.
   People talking without speaking,
   People hearing without listening,
   People writing songs that voices never share,
   And no one dare disturb the sound of silence.

4. "Fools!" said I, "You do not know.
   Silence like a cancer grows.
   Hear my words that I might teach you.
   Take my arms that I might reach you."
   But my words, like silent raindrops, fell
   And echoed in the wells of silence.

5. And the people bowed and prayed
   To the neon god they made.
   And the sign flashed out its warning
   In the words that it was forming.
   And the sign said, "The words of the prophets are
   Written on the subway walls
   And tenement halls." Whisper the sounds of silence.

Rock Around the Clock

Words and Music by Max C. Freedman and Jimmy DeKnight

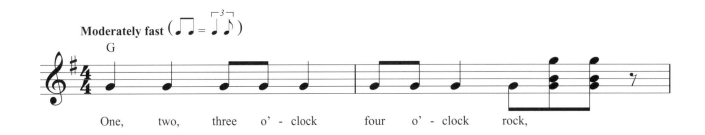

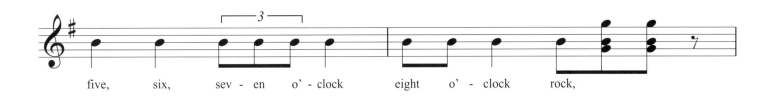

One, two, three o'-clock four o'-clock rock,

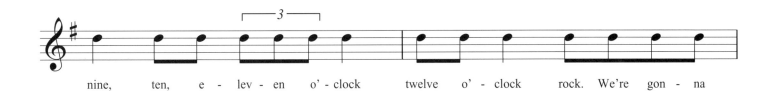

five, six, sev-en o'-clock eight o'-clock rock,

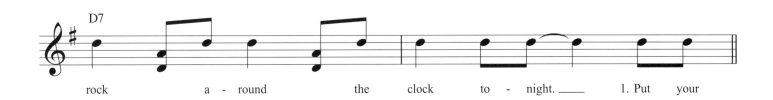

nine, ten, e-lev-en o'-clock twelve o'-clock rock. We're gon-na

rock a-round the clock to-night. ___ 1. Put your

glad rags on, join me, hon; ___ we'll have some fun when the

2.-5. See additional lyrics

clock strikes one. We're gon-na rock a-round the clock to-night. _ We're gon-na

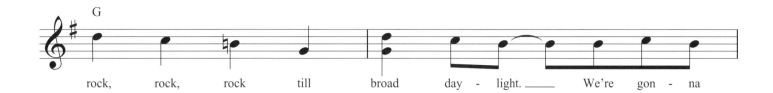

rock, rock, rock till broad day - light. _____ We're gon - na

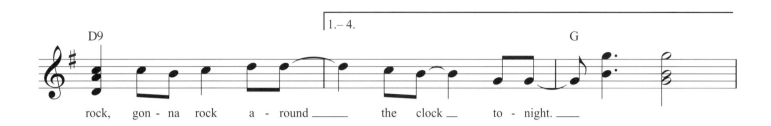

rock, gon - na rock a - round _____ the clock _ to - night. _____

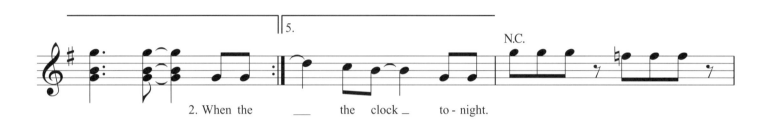

2. When the _____ the clock _ to - night.

Additional Lyrics

2. When the clock strikes two, three and four,
   If the band slows down we'll yell for more.
   We're gonna rock around the clock tonight.
   We're gonna rock, rock, rock till broad daylight.
   We're gonna rock, gonna rock around the clock tonight.

3. When the chimes ring five, six and seven,
   We'll be right in seventh heaven.
   We're gonna rock around the clock tonight.
   We're gonna rock, rock, rock till broad daylight.
   We're gonna rock, gonna rock around the clock tonight.

4. When it's eight, nine, ten, eleven too,
   I'll be goin' strong and so will you.
   We're gonna rock around the clock tonight.
   We're gonna rock, rock, rock till broad daylight.
   We're gonna rock, gonna rock around the clock tonight.

5. When the clock strikes twelve, we'll cool off then,
   Start a rockin' 'round the clock again.
   We're gonna rock around the clock tonight.
   We're gonna rock, rock, rock till broad daylight.
   We're gonna rock, gonna rock around the clock tonight.

I Will Always Love You

Words and Music by Dolly Parton

God Only Knows

Words and Music by Brian Wilson and Tony Asher

Stand by Me

Words and Music by Jerry Leiber, Mike Stoller and Ben E. King

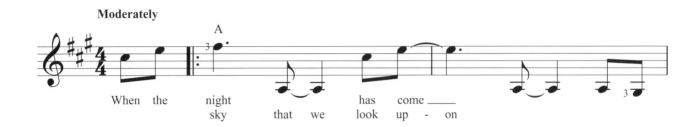

me. So dar - ling, dar - ling, stand by

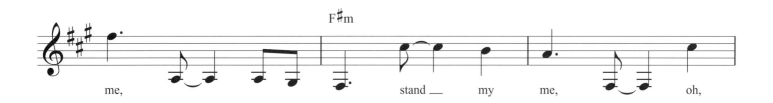

me, stand ___ my me, oh,

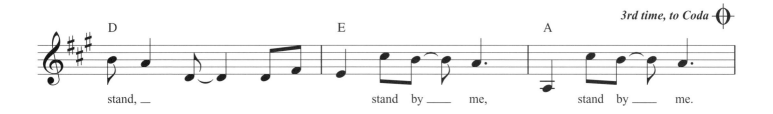

stand, ___ stand by ___ me, stand by ___ me.

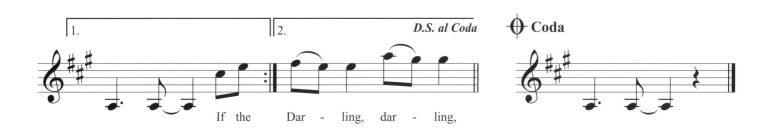

If the Dar - ling, dar - ling,

Ring of Fire

Words and Music by Merle Kilgore and June Carter

Love
taste

is   a   burn - ing   thing
of   love   is   thing   sweet

and   it   makes
when   hearts

a   fier - y   ring.
like   ours ____ meet.

Bound by wild de - sire,
I fell for you like a child.

I fell in - to a
Oh, but the

ring of fire.
fire went fire. wild.
I fell

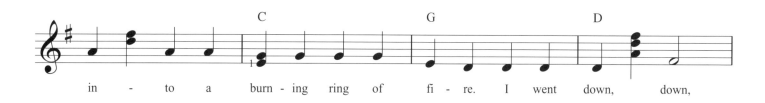

in - to a burn - ing ring of fi - re. I went down, down,

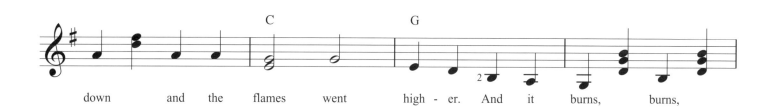

down and the flames went high - er. And it burns, burns,

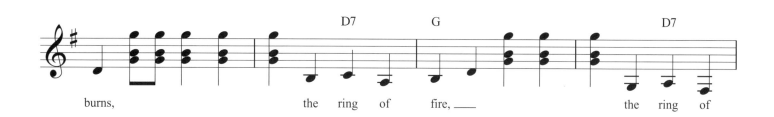

burns, the ring of fire, ___ the ring of

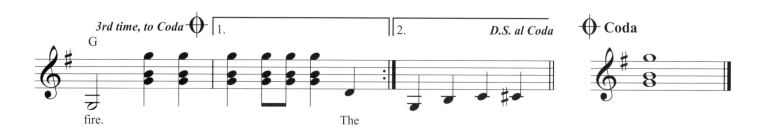

fire. The

My Favorite Things

from THE SOUND OF MUSIC

Lyrics by Oscar Hammerstein II
Music by Richard Rodgers

Rain - drops on ros - es and whis - kers on kit - tens,
Cream - col - ored po - nies and crisp ap - ple stru - dels,

bright cop - per ket - tles and warm wool - en mit - tens,
door - bells and sleigh - bells and schnit - zel with noo - dles,

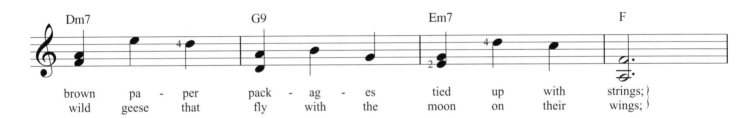

brown pa - per pack - ag - es tied up with strings;
wild geese that fly with the moon on their wings;

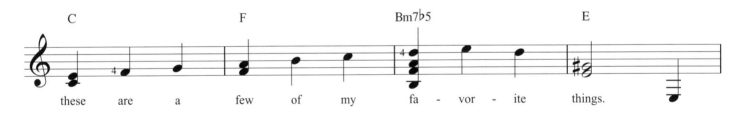

these are a few of my fa - vor - ite things.

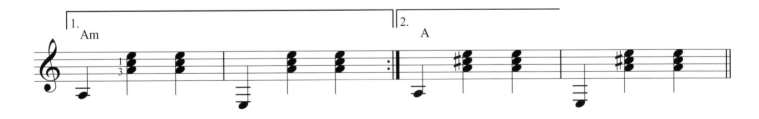

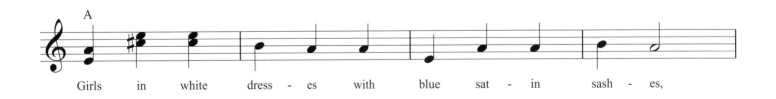

Girls in white dress - es with blue sat - in sash - es,

snow - flakes that stay on my nose and eye - lash - es,

sil - ver white win - ters that melt in - to springs;

these are a few of my fa - vor - ite things.

When the dog bites, when the bee stings,

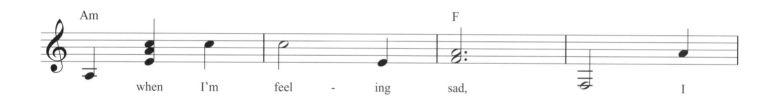

when I'm feel - ing sad, I

sim - ply re - mem - ber my fa - vor - ite things and

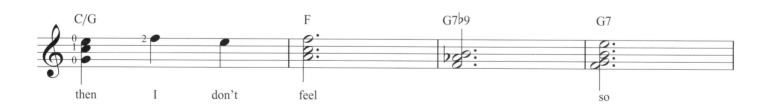

then I don't feel so

bad.

Edelweiss

from THE SOUND OF MUSIC

Lyrics by Oscar Hammerstein II
Music by Richard Rodgers

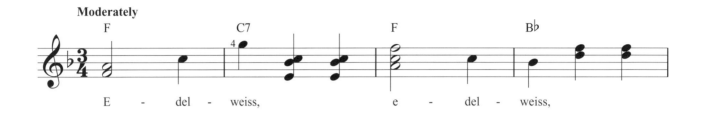

E - del - weiss, e - del - weiss,

ev - 'ry morn - ing you greet me.

Small and white, clean and bright,

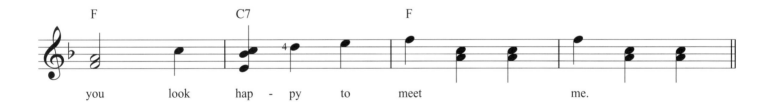

you look hap - py to meet me.

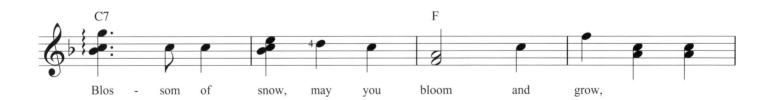

Blos - som of snow, may you bloom and grow,

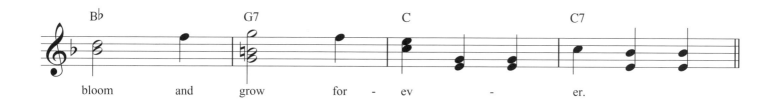

bloom and grow for - ev - er.

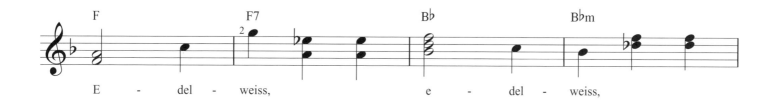

E - del - weiss, e - del - weiss,

bless my home - land for - ev - er.

Hey, Soul Sister

Words and Music by Pat Monahan, Espen Lind and Amund Bjorklund

lid - ed you're the one I have de - cid - ed who's one of my kind. __
you; like a vir - gin, you're Ma - don - na, and I'm al - ways gon - na

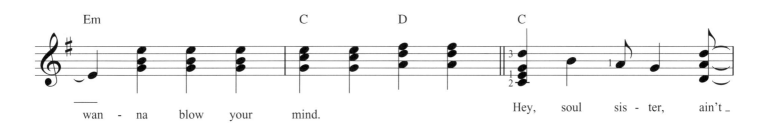

wan - na blow your mind. Hey, soul sis - ter, ain't _

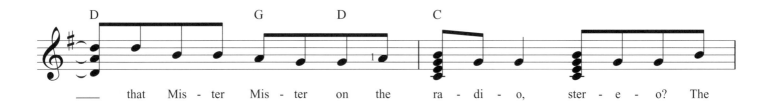

__ that Mis - ter Mis - ter on the ra - di - o, ster - e - o? The

way you move ain't fair, you know. Hey, soul sis - ter, I ____

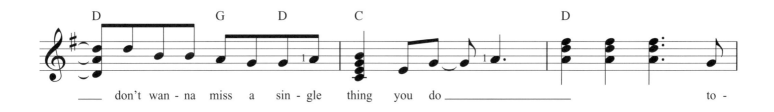

__ don't wan - na miss a sin - gle thing you do _____ to -

night. Hey, _____ hey, _____ hey. _____

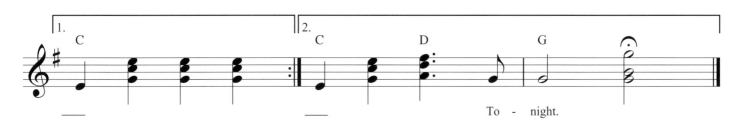

__ To - night.

People Get Ready

Words and Music by Curtis Mayfield

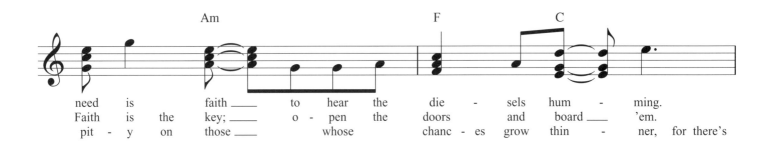

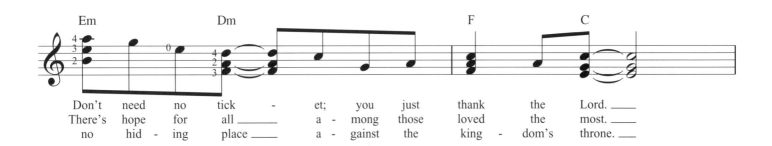

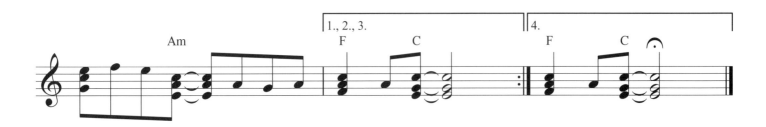

Me and Bobby McGee

Words and Music by Kris Kristofferson and Fred Foster

Moderately, in 2

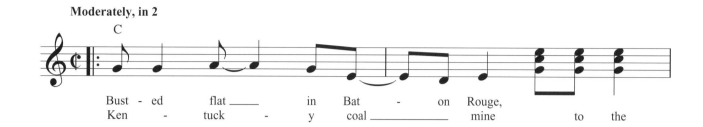

Bust - ed flat ___ in Bat - on Rouge,
Ken - tuck - y coal ___ mine to the

wait - in' ___ for a train, ___ when I was feel - in' near ___ as
Cal - i - for - nia sun, ___ hey, Bob - by shared ___ the

fad - ed as my jeans.
se - crets of my soul. Through

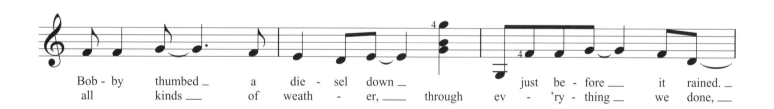

Bob - by thumbed ___ a die - sel down ___ just be - fore ___ it rained. ___
all kinds ___ of weath - er, ___ through ev - 'ry - thing ___ we done, ___

___ It rode us all ___ the way in to New Or -
___ yeah, Bob - by, ba - by, kept me from the

leans. / cold.   I pulled my har - poon
One day near Sa - li -

out of my dirt - y red ___ ban - dan - na. ___ I was
- as, Lord, I let him slip ___ a - way. _____ He's

play - in' soft while Bob - by sang the blues. ___
look - in' for that home and I hope he finds it.

But I'd   Wind - shield wip - ers slap - pin' time, ___ I was
trade all of my to - mor - rows   for one

hold - in' ___ Bob - by's hand ___ in mine.   We sang ev - 'ry song ___
sin - gle ___ yes - ter - day, ___   to be hold - in' Bob - by's bod -

___ that driv - er knew. ___
- y next to mine. ___

Free - dom's just an - oth - er word for noth - in' left to lose. ___

___ Noth- in', I mean noth - in', hon', if it ain't
and that's all _____ that Bob - by left

free. _____ Yeah, feel - in' good was
me. _____

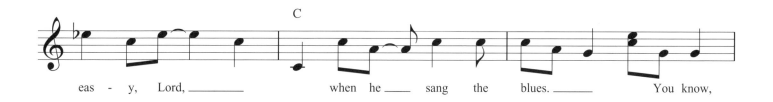

eas - y, Lord, _____ when he ___ sang the blues. _____ You know,

feel - in' good was good e - nough ___ for me, _____

good e - nough ___ for me _____ an' my Bob - by Mc -

Gee. From the

Fields of Gold

Music and Lyrics by Sting

You'll re - mem - ber me ___ when the west wind moves _ up -
stay with me, ___ will you be my love ___ a -
years have passed _ since those sum - mer days ___ a -

on the fields _ of bar - ley. You'll for - get the sun ___ in his
mong the fields _ of bar - ley? We'll for - get the sun ___ in his
mong the fields _ of bar - ley. See the chil - dren run ___ as the

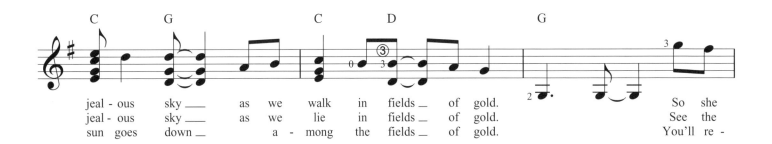

jeal - ous sky ___ as we walk in fields _ of gold. So she
jeal - ous sky ___ as we lie in fields _ of gold. See the
sun goes down ___ a - mong the fields _ of gold. You'll re -

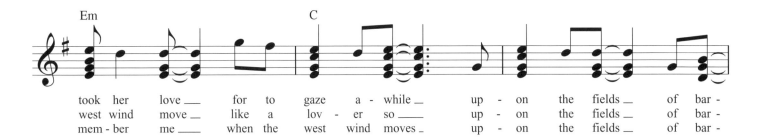

took her love ___ for to gaze a - while ___ up - on the fields _ of bar -
west wind move ___ like a lov - er so ___ up - on the fields _ of bar -
mem - ber me ___ when the west wind moves _ up - on the fields _ of bar -

3rd time, to Coda ⊕

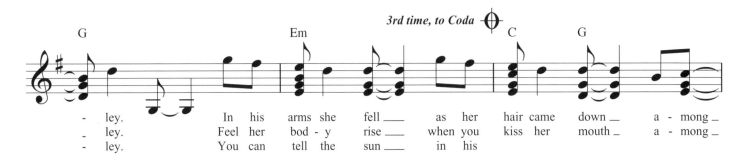

- ley. In his arms she fell ___ as her hair came down ___ a - mong ___
- ley. Feel her bod - y rise ___ when you kiss her mouth ___ a - mong ___
- ley. You can tell the sun ___ in his

Hotel California

Words and Music by Don Henley, Glenn Frey and Don Felder

such a love - ly face. ___ They're

Plen - ty of room ___ at the Ho - tel Cal - i - for - nia.
liv - in' it up ___ at the Ho - tel Cal - i - for - nia.

An - y time ___ of year, ___ you can
What a nice ___ sur - prise; ___ bring your

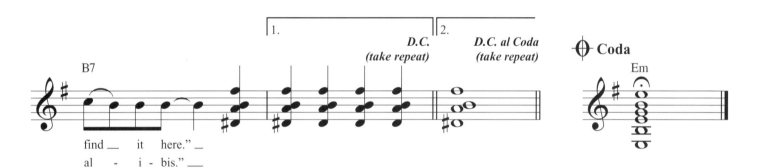

find ___ it here." ___
al - i - bis." ___

1. D.C. (take repeat) 2. D.C. al Coda (take repeat) Coda

Additional Lyircs

2. There she stood in the doorway; I heard the mission bell.
   And I was thinking to myself, "This could be heaven or this could be hell."
   Then she lit up a candle and she showed me the way.
   There were voices down the corridor; I thought I heard them say:

3. Her mind is Tiffany twisted; she got the Mercedes bends.
   She got a lot of pretty, pretty boys that she calls friends.
   How they dance in the courtyard; sweet summer sweat.
   Some dance to remember, some dance to forget.

4. So I called up the captain: "Please bring me my wine."
   He said, "We haven't had that spirit here since nineteen sixty-nine."
   And still those voices are calling from far away;
   Wake you up in the middle of the night just to hear them say:

5. Mirrors on the ceiling, the pink champagne on ice,
   And she said, "We are all just prisoners here of our own device."
   And in the master's chambers they gathered for the feast.
   They stab it with their steely knives, but they just can't kill the beast.

6. Last thing I remember, I was running for the door.
   I had to find the passage back to the place I was before.
   "Relax," said the night man. "We are programmed to receive.
   You can check out any time you like, but you can never leave."

Can't Help Falling in Love

from the Paramount Picture BLUE HAWAII

Words and Music by George David Weiss, Hugo Peretti and Luigi Creatore

Brown Eyed Girl

Words and Music by Van Morrison

Moderately

1. Hey, where did we __
2., 3. *See additional lyrics*

__ go?   Days when the rains __ came,

down in the hol-low,   play-ing a new __

__ game,   laugh-ing and a run-ning, hey, hey,

skip - ping and a jump - ing

in the mist - y

morn - ing fog with our

hearts a thump - ing, and

you,

my brown - eyed girl,

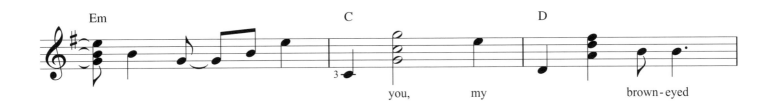

you, my

brown - eyed

1.

girl.

2.

Do you re - mem - ber when

we used to sing:

Sha, la, la, la, la, la, la, la, la, la, te, da.

Sha, la, la, la, la, la, la, la,

Fine

la, la, la, te, da, la, te, da.

D.S. al Fine
(take 2nd ending)

Additional Lyrics

2. Whatever happened to Tuesday and so slow,
   Going down the old mine with a transistor radio,
   Standing in the sunlight laughing,
   Hiding behind a rainbow's wall,
   Slipping and a sliding
   All along the waterfall
   With you, my brown-eyed girl,
   You, my brown-eyed girl.
   Do you remember when we used to sing:

3. So hard to find my way, now that I'm all on my own.
   I saw you just the other day; my, how you have grown.
   Cast my memory back there, Lord.
   Sometimes I'm overcome thinking 'bout
   Making love in the green grass
   Behind the stadium
   With you, my brown-eyed girl,
   You, my brown-eyed girl.
   Do you remember when we used to sing:

Let It Go

from Disney's Animated Feature FROZEN

Music and Lyrics by Kristen Anderson-Lopez and Robert Lopez

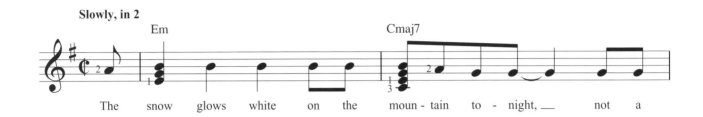

The snow glows white on the moun-tain to-night, _____ not a

foot-print _____ to be seen. _____ A king-dom of i - so - la -

- tion, _____ and it looks like _____ I'm the queen. _____

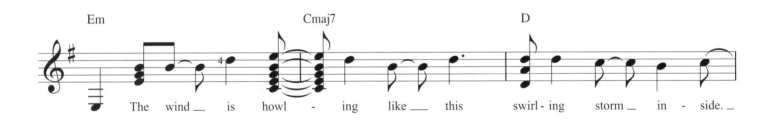

The wind _ is howl - ing like _ this swirl-ing storm _ in - side. _

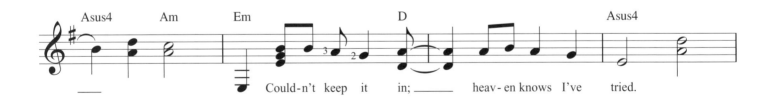

_____ Could-n't keep it in; _____ heav-en knows I've tried.

Don't let _ them in, _____ don't let _ them see. _____

Happy Together

Words and Music by Garry Bonner and Alan Gordon

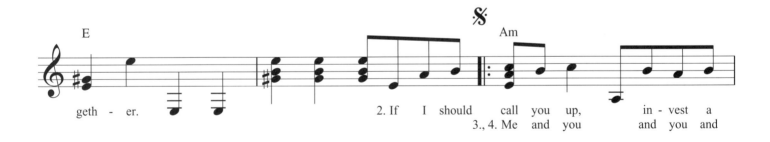

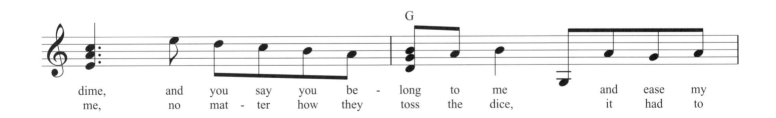

mind,   i - mag - ine how the world could be: so ver - y
be.   The on - ly one for me is you,   and you for

To Coda ⊕

fine.   So hap - py to - geth - er.
me.

I can see me lov - in' no - bod - y but you for all my life.

When you're with me, ba - by, the skies will be

2nd time, D.S. al Coda   ⊕ **Coda**

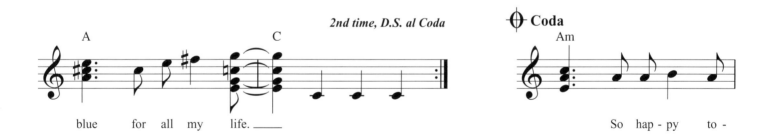

blue for all my life.   So hap - py to -

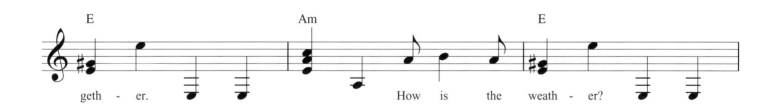

geth - er.   How is the weath - er?

So hap - py to - geth - er.

I Want to Hold Your Hand

Words and Music by John Lennon and Paul McCartney

And when I touch you, I feel hap-py in-side. _

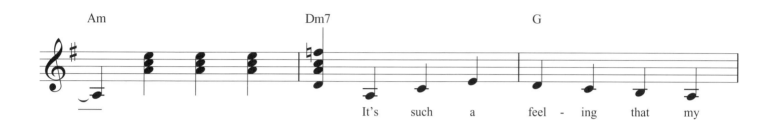

It's such a feel-ing that my

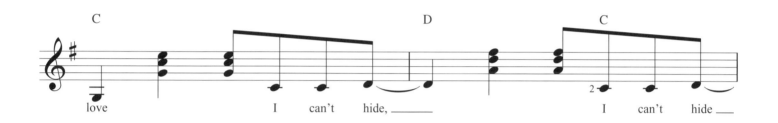

love I can't hide, _____ I can't hide ___

D.S. al Coda

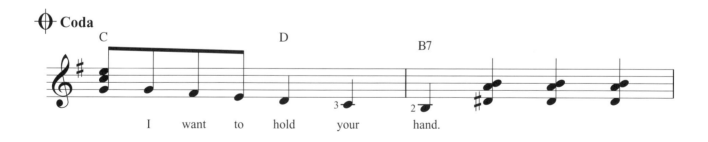

___ I can't hide. ___ Yeah,

Coda

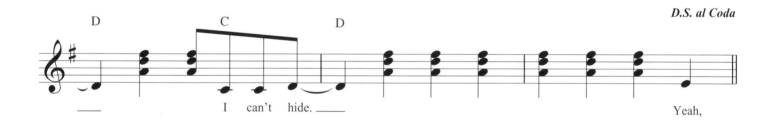

I want to hold your hand.

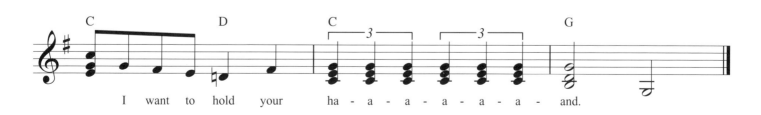

I want to hold your ha - a - a - a - a - a - and.

I'm a Believer

Words and Music by Neil Diamond

Moderately fast

I thought love was on - ly true in
I thought love was more or less a

fair - y tales,
giv - in' thing;
meant for some - one
seems the more I

else but not for me.
gave the less I got.

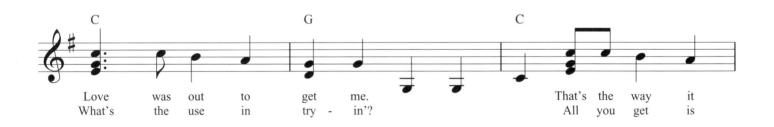

Love was out to get me.
What's the use in try - in'?
That's the way it
All you get is

seemed.
pain.
Dis - ap - point - ment haunt - ed all my
When I need - ed sun - shine, I got

dreams. }
rain. }

Then I saw her face.

Now I'm ___ a be - liev - er.

Not a

trace

of doubt ___ in my mind.

I'm in love.

I'm ___ a be -

liev - er. I could - n't leave her if I tried.

1.

2.

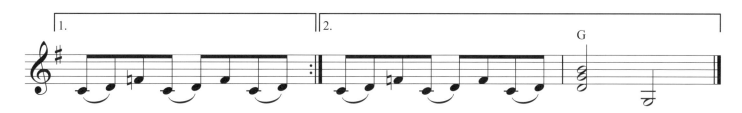

I'm Yours

Words and Music by Jason Mraz

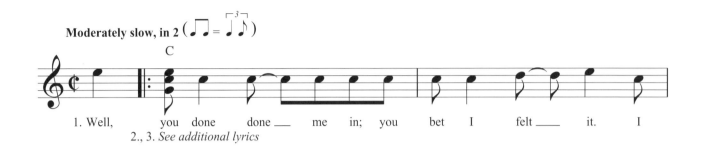

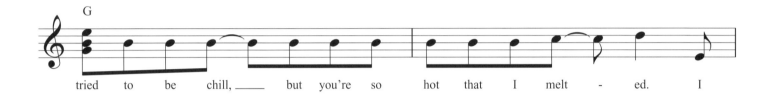

1. Well, you done done __ me in; you bet I felt __ it. I
2., 3. *See additional lyrics*

tried to be chill, __ but you're so hot that I melt - ed. I

fell right through __ the cracks — Now I'm try - ing to get __ back.

Be - fore the cool done run out, I'll be giv - ing it my best - est, and

noth - ing's gon - na stop me but di - vine in - ter - ven - tion. I

reck - on it's a - gain my turn _____ to win some __ or

learn __ some. But I won't hes - i - tate no

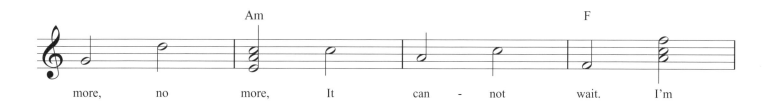

more, no more, It can - not wait. I'm

yours. _____

3. I've been __ spend-ing

Additional Lyrics

2. Well, open up your mind and see like me.
   Open up your plans and, damn, you're free.
   Look into your heart and you'll find
   Love, love, love, love.
   Listen to the music of the moment.
   People dance and sing; we're just one big family,
   And it's our Godforsaken right to be
   Loved, loved, loved, loved, loved.

3. I've been spending way too long checking my tongue in the mirror
   And bending over backwards just to try to see it clearer,
   But my breath fogged up the glass
   And so I drew a new face and I laughed.
   I guess what I'll be saying is there ain't no better reason
   To rid yourself of vanities and just go with the seasons.
   It's what we aim to do.
   Our name is our virtue.

California Dreamin'

Words and Music by John Phillips and Michelle Phillips

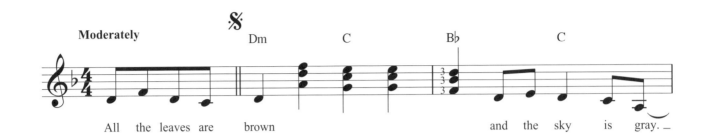

All the leaves are brown and the sky is gray.

I've been for a walk

on a win-ter's day. I'd be safe and / If I did-n't

warm / tell her if I was in L. A. / I could leave to-day.

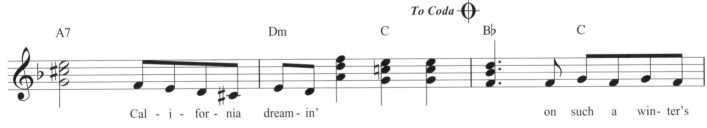

To Coda

Cal-i-for-nia dream-in' on such a win-ter's

day. Stopped in-to a church

I passed a - long the way. Well, I got down on my

knees and I pre - tend to pray. ____

You know, the preach - er, like the cold; ____

he knows I'm gon - na stay. Cal - i - for - nia

dream - in' on such a win - ter's day.

D.S. al Coda

Coda

All the leaves are

on such a win - ter's

day, on such a win - ter's day,

on such a win - ter's day.

In My Life

Words and Music by John Lennon and Paul McCartney

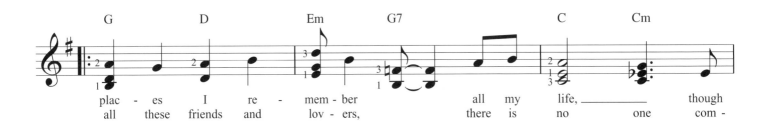

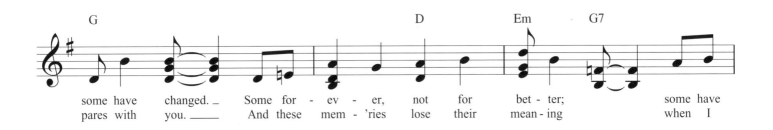

dead ___ and ___ some ___ are ___ liv - ing. In my ___ life I've
know I'll of - ten stop and think a - bout them. In my ___ life I

loved them all. ___ But of
love you more. ___

Lean on Me

Words and Music by Bill Withers

if I have things ____ you need to bor - row, ____

you have to bear ____ that you can't car - ry, ____

for no one can fill ____ those of your needs ____ that you won't let ____

I'm right up the road; ____ I'll share your load ____ if you just call ____

____ show. __ You just call on me, broth - er, when you need a hand. __ We all ____

need some-bod - y to lean ____ on. __ I just might have a prob - lem that

you'll un - der - stand. __ We all __ need some - bod - y to lean __

____ on. __ Lean on me.

Coda

____ me. __ Call __ me. __

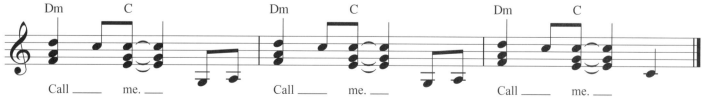

Call __ me. __ Call ____ me. __ Call __ me. __

Tomorrow

from the Musical Production ANNIE

Lyric by Martin Charnin
Music by Charles Strouse

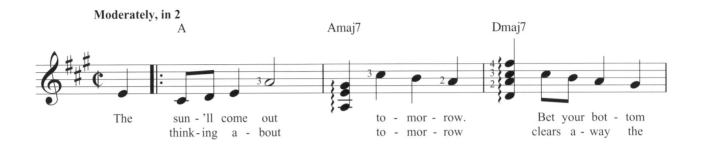

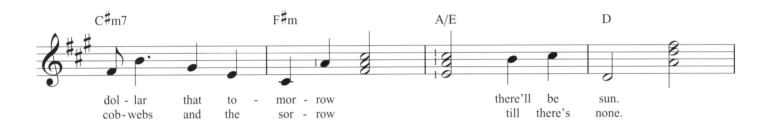

The sun-'ll come out to-mor-row. Bet your bot-tom
think-ing a-bout to-mor-row clears a-way the

dol-lar that to-mor-row there'll be sun.
cob-webs and the sor-row till there's none.

Just
When I'm stuck with a day that's

gray and lone-ly, I just stick out my chin and

grin and say:

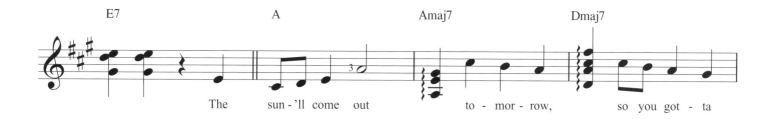

The sun-'ll come out to-mor-row, so you got-ta

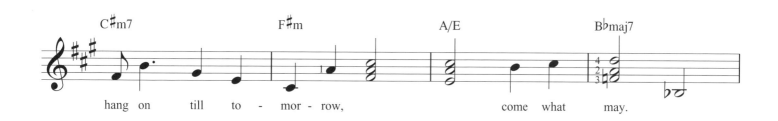

hang on till to-mor-row, come what may.

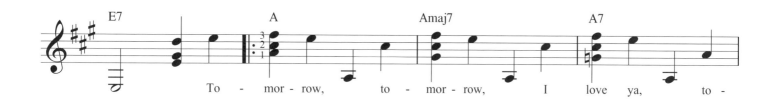

To-mor-row, to-mor-row, I love ya, to-

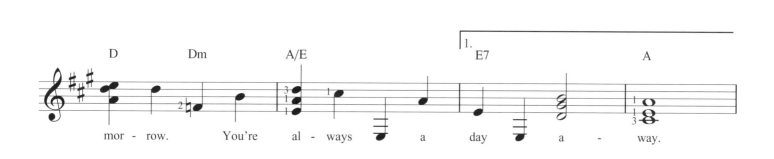

mor-row. You're al-ways a day a-way.

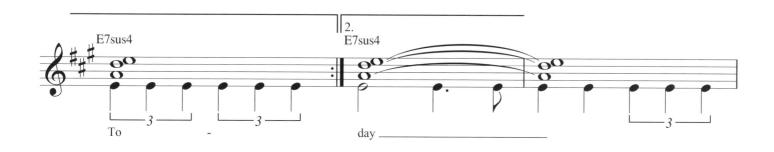

To - day

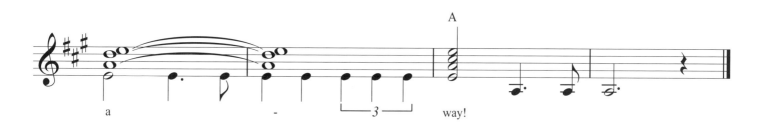

a - way!

My Heart Will Go On

(Love Theme from 'Titanic')

from the Paramount and Twentieth Century Fox Motion Picture TITANIC

Music by James Horner
Lyric by Will Jennings

Ev - 'ry night in my dreams, I see you, I
Love can touch us one time and last for a

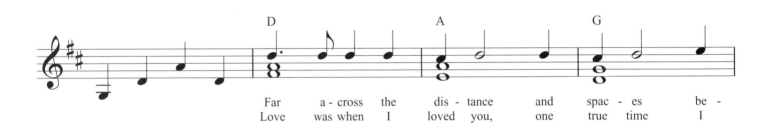

feel you. That is how I know you go on.
life - time and nev - er let go till we're gone.

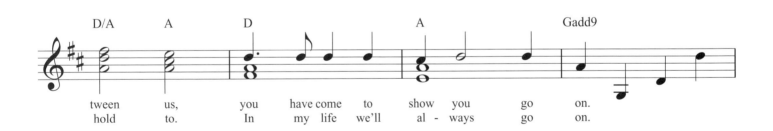

Far a - cross the dis - tance and spac - es be -
Love was when I loved you, one true time I

tween us, you have come to show you go on.
hold to. In my life we'll al - ways go on.

1., 2. Near, far, wher - ev - er you
3. You're here; there's noth - ing I

are,   I   be - lieve   that   the   heart does   go   on. _____

fear,   and   I   know   that   my   heart will   go   on. _____

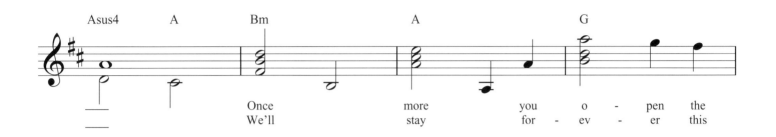

_____   Once   more   you   o - pen   the

_____   We'll   stay   for - ev - er   this

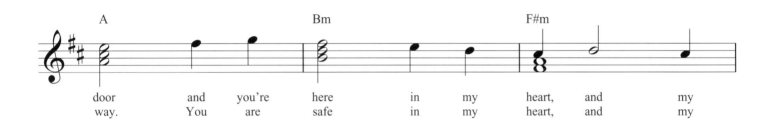

door   and you're   here   in   my   heart, and   my

way.   You   are   safe   in   my   heart, and   my

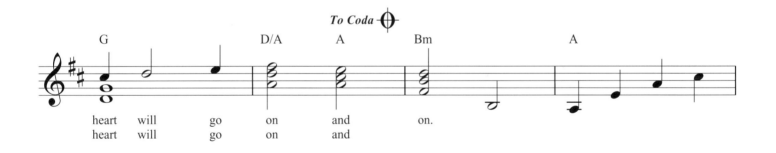

heart will   go   on   and   on.

heart will   go   on   and

on.

Hallelujah

Words and Music by Leonard Cohen

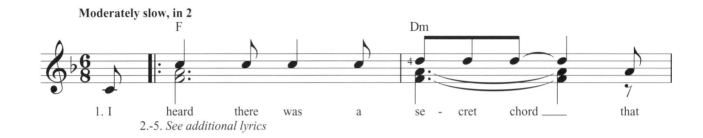

Moderately slow, in 2

1. I heard there was a se - cret chord ___ that

2.-5. *See additional lyrics*

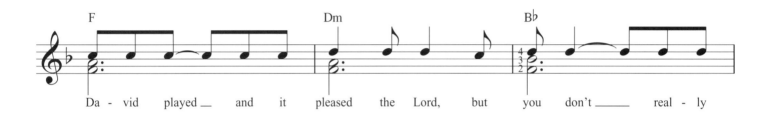

Da - vid played ___ and it pleased the Lord, but you don't ___ real - ly

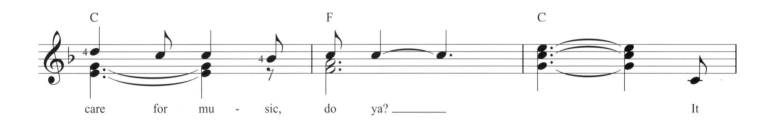

care for mu - sic, do ya? ___ It

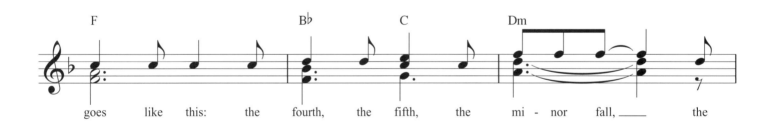

goes like this: the fourth, the fifth, the mi - nor fall, ___ the

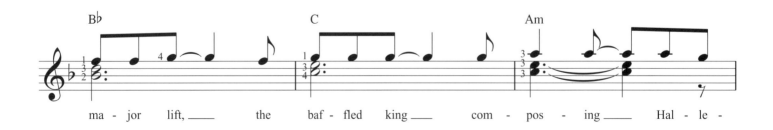

ma - jor lift, ___ the baf - fled king ___ com - pos - ing ___ Hal - le -

lu - jah. _____ Hal - le - lu - jah, hal - le -

lu - jah, hal - le - lu - jah, hal - le - lu -

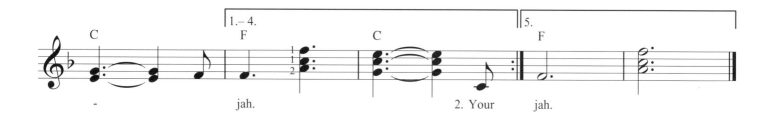

- jah. 2. Your jah.

Additional Lyrics

2. Your faith was strong but you needed proof.
   You saw her bathing on the roof.
   Her beauty and the moonlight overthrew ya.
   She tied you to a kitchen chair.
   She broke your throne, she cut your hair,
   And from your lips she drew the Hallelujah.

3. Maybe I have been here before.
   I know this room, I've walked this floor.
   I used to live alone before I knew ya.
   I've seen your flag on the marble arch.
   Love is not a victory march.
   It's a cold and it's a broken Hallelujah.

4. There was a time you let me know
   What's real and going on below.
   But now you never show it to me, do ya?
   And remember when I moved in you.
   The holy dark was movin' too,
   And every breath we drew was Hallelujah.

5. Maybe there's a God above,
   And all I ever learned from love
   Was how to shoot at someone who outdrew ya.
   And it's not a cry you can hear at night.
   It's not somebody who's seen the light.
   It's a cold and it's a broken Hallelujah.

Yesterday

Words and Music by John Lennon and Paul McCartney

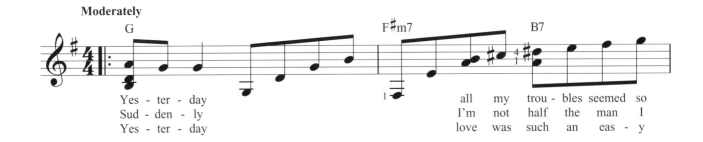

Yes - ter - day   all   my   trou - bles   seemed   so
Sud - den - ly   I'm   not   half   the   man   I
Yes - ter - day   love   was   such   an   eas - y

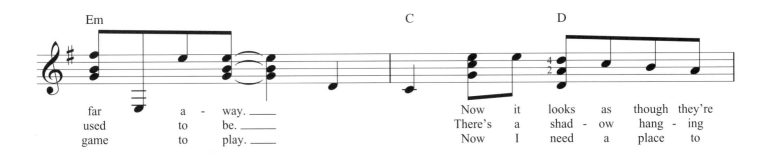

far   a - way.   Now   it   looks   as   though   they're
used   to   be.   There's   a   shad - ow   hang - ing
game   to   play.   Now   I   need   a   place   to

here   to   stay.   Oh,   I   be - lieve   in
o - ver   me.   Oh,   yes - ter - day   came
hide   a - way.   Oh,   I   be - lieve   in

3rd time, to Coda

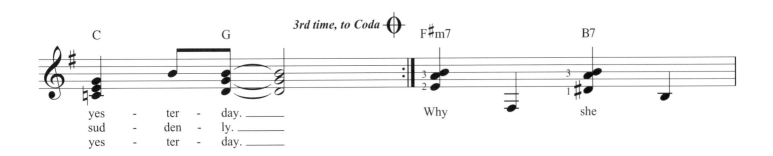

yes - ter - day.   Why   she
sud - den - ly.
yes - ter - day.

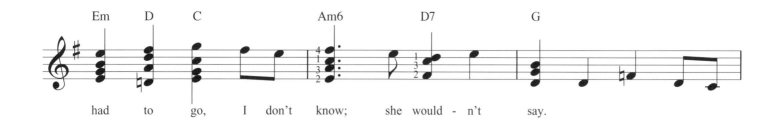

had to go, I don't know; she would - n't say.

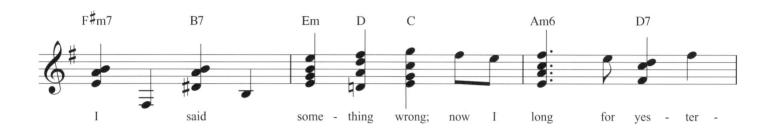

I said some - thing wrong; now I long for yes - ter -

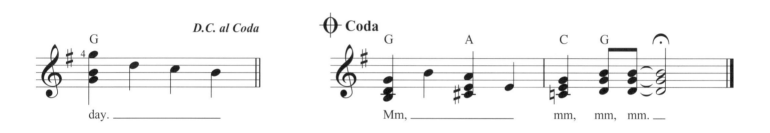

D.C. al Coda

day. _____

Coda

Mm, _____ mm, mm, mm. _____

More
(Ti Guarderò Nel Cuore)

from the film MONDO CANE

Music by Nino Oliviero and Riz Ortolani
Italian Lyrics by Marcello Ciorciolini
English Lyrics by Norman Newell

Star Wars
(Main Theme)
from STAR WARS, THE EMPIRE STRIKES BACK and RETURN OF THE JEDI

Music by John Williams

Moon River

from the Paramount Picture BREAKFAST AT TIFFANY'S

Words by Johnny Mercer
Music by Henry Mancini

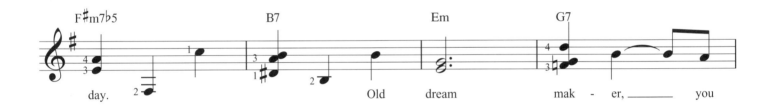

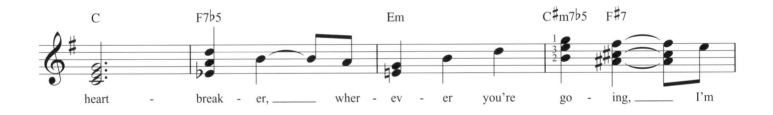

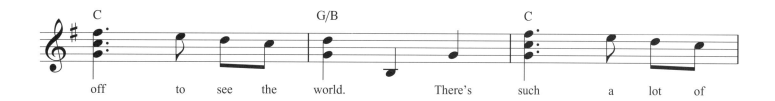

off   to   see the   world.   There's   such   a lot of

world   to   see.   We're

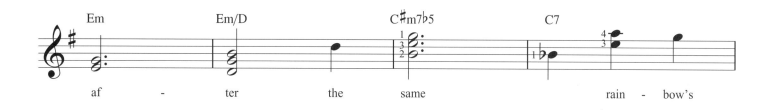

af - ter   the   same   rain - bow's

end,   wait - ing 'round the bend,

my huck - le - ber - ry   friend,   Moon

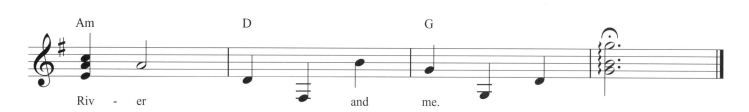

Riv - er   and   me.

Sunrise, Sunset

from the Musical FIDDLER ON THE ROOF

Words by Sheldon Harnick
Music by Jerry Bock

Moderately

Is this the lit-tle girl I car - ried?
When did she get to be a beau - ty?

Is this the lit-tle boy at play?
When did he grow to be so tall?

I don't re - mem - ber grow - ing old - er.
Was - n't it yes - ter - day when old they

When did they?

were small?

Sun - rise, sun - set, sun - rise,

sun - set,   swift - ly   { flow   the   days.
                                { fly   the   years.

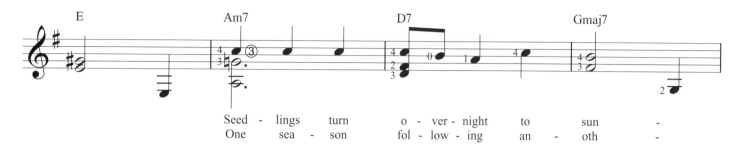

Seed - lings   turn   o - ver - night   to   sun -
One   sea - son   fol - low - ing   an - oth -

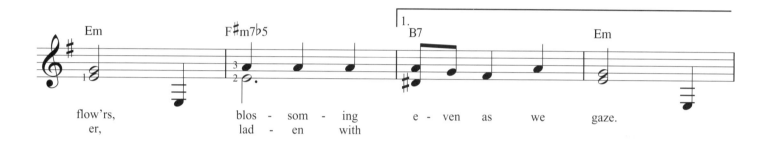

flow'rs,   blos - som - ing   e - ven   as   we   gaze.
er,   lad - en   with

hap - pi - ness   and   tears.

My Cherie Amour

Words and Music by Stevie Wonder, Sylvia Moy and Henry Cosby

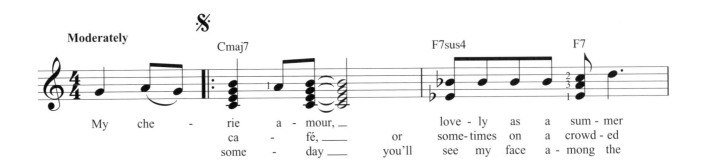

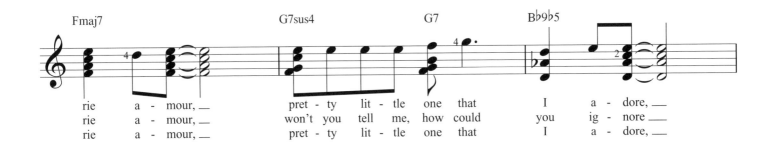

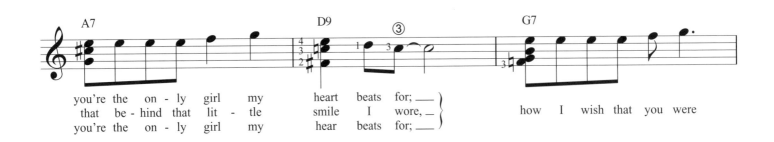

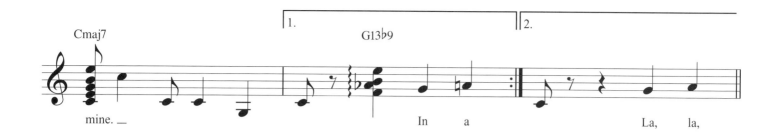

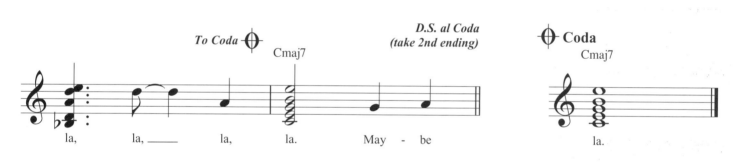

The Way You Look Tonight

Words by Dorothy Fields
Music by Jerome Kern

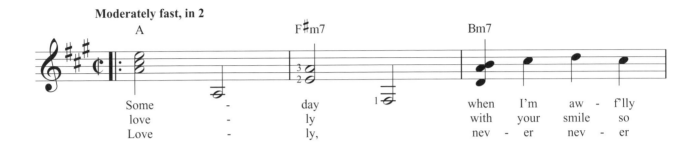

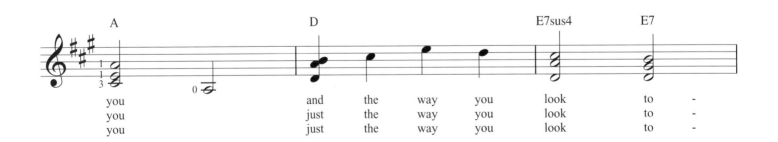

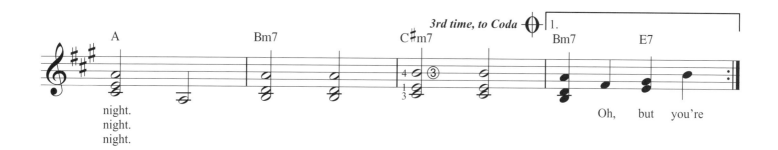

night.
night.
night.

Oh, but you're

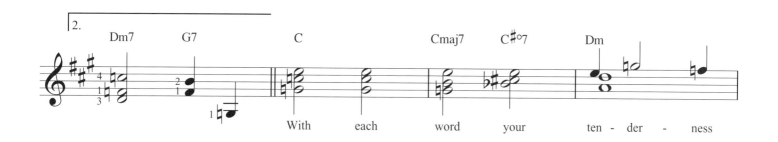

With each word your ten - der - ness

grows, tear - ing my fear a - part. _____

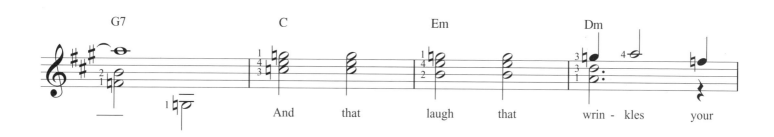

And that laugh that wrin - kles your

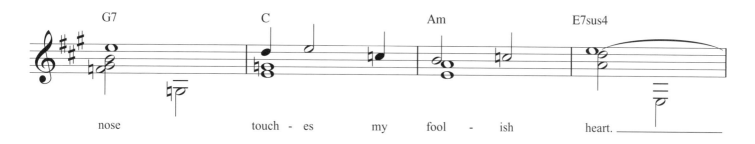

nose touch - es my fool - ish heart. _____

Let It Be

Words and Music by John Lennon and Paul McCartney

Moderately slow

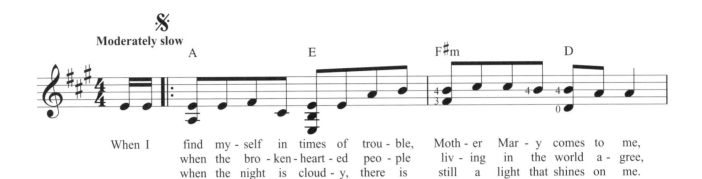

When I find my-self in times of trou - ble, Moth - er Mar - y comes to me,
when the bro - ken-heart - ed peo - ple liv - ing in the world a - gree,
when the night is cloud - y, there is still a light that shines on me.

speak - ing words of wis - dom Let it be. ____ And
there will be an an - swer. Let it be. ____ For
Shine on till to - mor - row. Let it be. ____ I

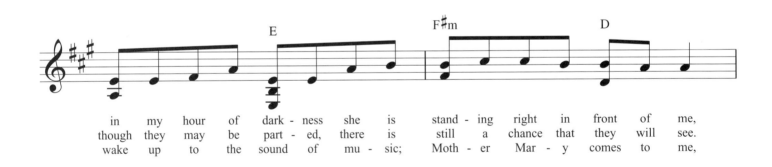

in my hour of dark - ness she is stand - ing right in front of me,
though they may be part - ed, there is still a chance that they will see.
wake up to the sound of mu - sic; Moth - er Mar - y comes to me,

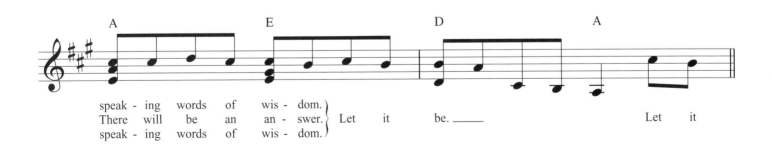

speak - ing words of wis - dom.
There will be an an - swer. } Let it be. ____ Let it
speak - ing words of wis - dom.

be, let it be, let it be, _____ let it be.

{ Whis - per words of wis - dom.
There will be an an - swer. } Let it be. _____ And
There will be an an - swer.

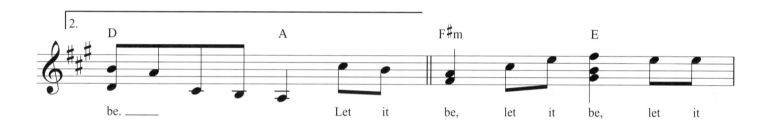

be. _____ Let it be, let it be, let it

be, _____ let it be. Whis - per words of wis - dom. Let it

Fine

be. ____

D.S. al Fine
(take 2nd ending)

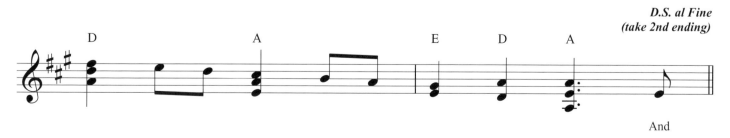

And

Every Breath You Take

Music and Lyrics by Sting

Ev - 'ry breath you __

take,
day,
make,

ev - 'ry move you __ make,
ev - 'ry word you __ say,
ev - 'ry vow you __ break,

ev - 'ry bond __ you break,
ev - 'ry game __ you play,
ev - 'ry smile __ you take,

ev - 'ry step __ you take,
ev - 'ry night __ you stay,
ev - 'ry claim __ you stake,

I'll be watch - ing you.
I'll be watch - ing you.
I'll be watch - ing you.

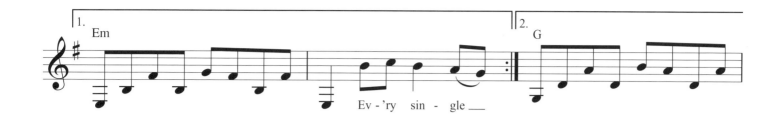

Ev - 'ry   sin - gle ___

Fine

Oh,   can't   you ___   see   you   be - long   to ___

me?   How   my   poor   heart ___   aches ___

D.S. al Fine
(take 2nd ending)

with   ev - 'ry   step ___   you   take.   Ev - 'ry   move   you ___

Crazy

Words and Music by Willie Nelson

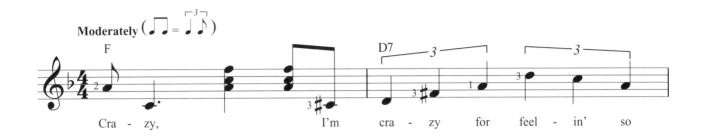

Cra - zy,   I'm cra - zy for feel - in' so

lone - ly.   I'm cra - zy,

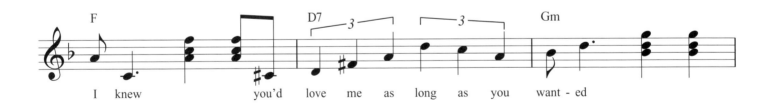

cra - zy for feel - in' so blue.

I knew   you'd love me as long as you want - ed

and then some - day   you'd leave me for some - bod - y

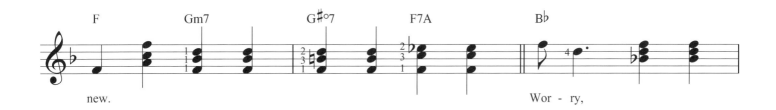

new.

Wor - ry,

why do I let my - self wor - ry,

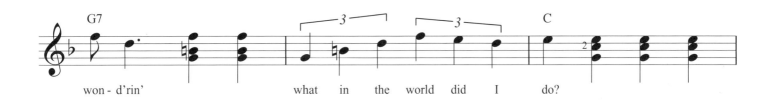

won - d'rin'   what in the world did I do?

Cra - zy   for think - ing that my love could

hold you.   I'm cra - zy for try - in' and

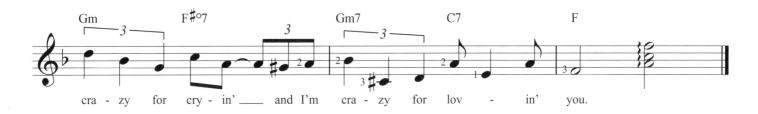

cra - zy for cry - in' ____ and I'm cra - zy for lov - in' you.

Space Oddity

Words and Music by David Bowie

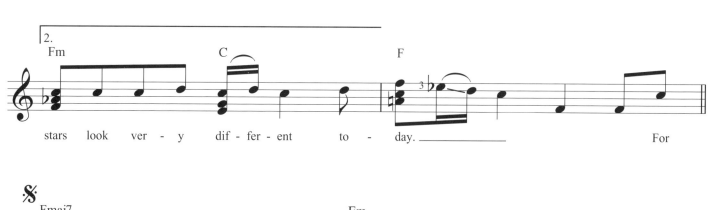

2.

Fm · C · F

stars look ver - y dif - fer - ent to - day. _____ For

Fmaj7 · Em

here · am I sit - ting in a tin can,
Here · am I float - ing 'round my tin can,

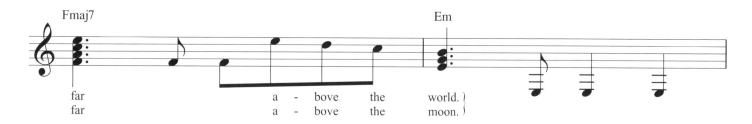

Fmaj7 · Em

far · a - bove the world. }
far · a - bove the moon. }

Fine

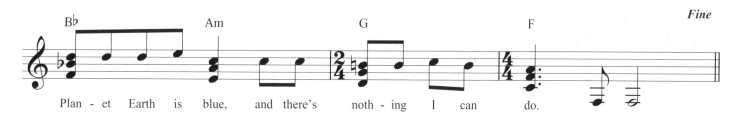

B♭ · Am · G · F

Plan - et Earth is blue, and there's noth - ing I can do.

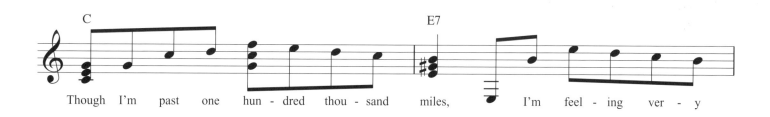

C · E7

Though I'm past one hun - dred thou - sand miles, I'm feel - ing ver - y

F · Fm · C

still. _____ And I think my space - ship knows which way to

F · Fm · C

go. _____ Tell my wife I love her ver - y much. She

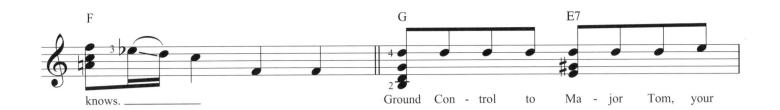

knows. _____

Ground Con - trol to Ma - jor Tom, your

cir - cuit's dead; there's some - thing wrong. Can you hear me, Ma - jor Tom? Can you

D.S. al Fine

hear me, Ma - jor Tom? Can you hear me, Ma - jor Tom? Can you...

When You Wish Upon a Star

Words by Ned Washington
Music by Leigh Harline

Tears in Heaven

Words and Music by Eric Clapton and Will Jennings

Georgia on My Mind

Words by Stuart Gorrell
Music by Hoagy Carmichael

When I Fall in Love

Words by Edward Heyman
Music by Victor Young

When I fall in love, it will be for-
When I give my heart, it will be com-

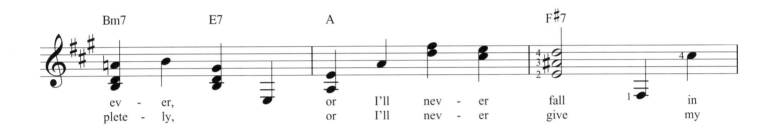

ev - er, or I'll nev - er fall in
plete - ly, or I'll nev - er give my

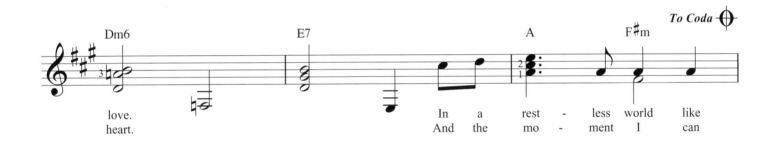

love.
heart.
In a rest - less world like
And the mo - ment I can

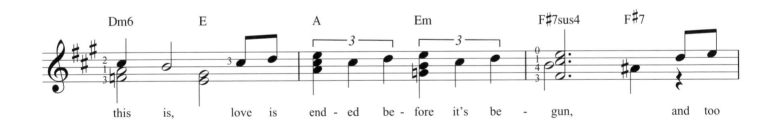

this is, love is end - ed be - fore it's be - gun, and too

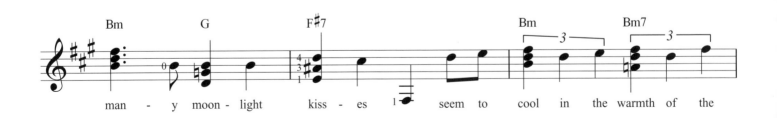

man - y moon - light kiss - es seem to cool in the warmth of the

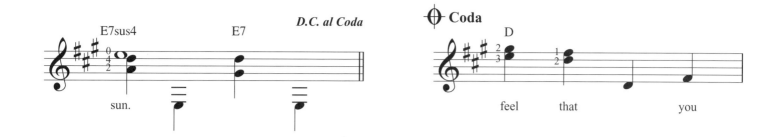

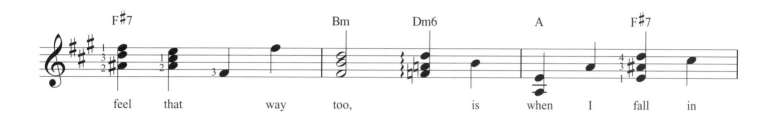

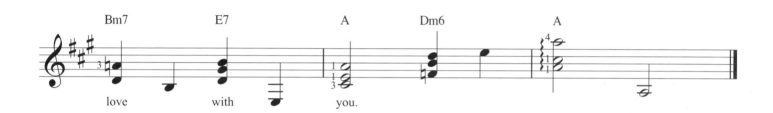

What a Wonderful World

Words and Music by George David Weiss and Bob Thiele

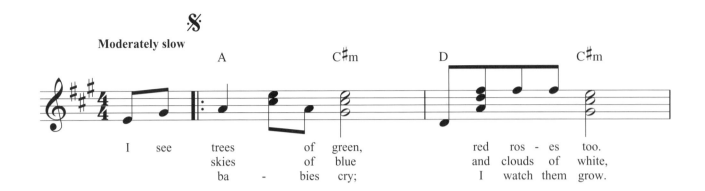

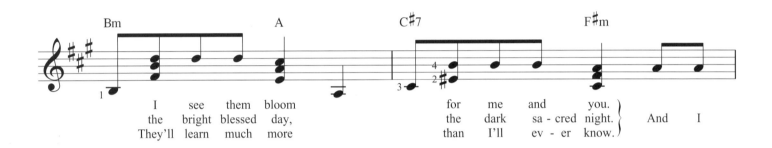

I see trees of green, red ros-es too.
skies of blue and clouds of white,
ba - bies cry; I watch them grow.

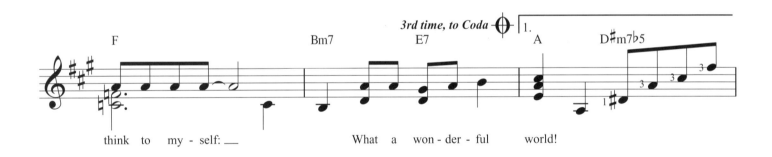

I see them bloom for me and you.
the bright blessed day, the dark sa - cred night. } And I
They'll learn much more than I'll ev - er know. }

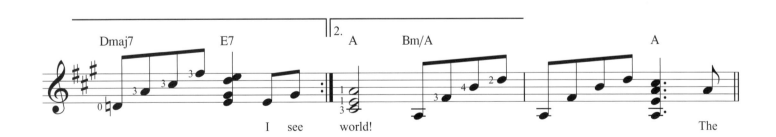

think to my - self: __ What a won-der-ful world!

I see world! The

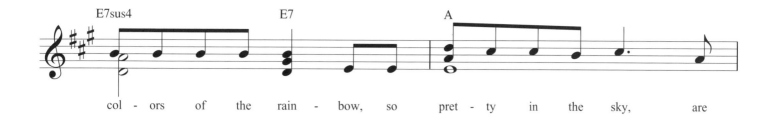

col - ors of the rain - bow, so pret - ty in the sky, are

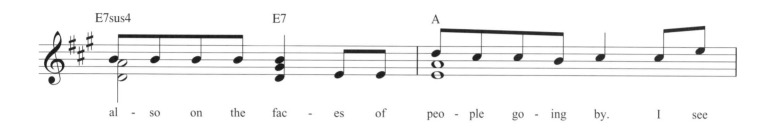

al - so on the fac - es of peo - ple go - ing by. I see

friends shak - ing hands, say - ing, "How do you do?"

D.S. al Coda

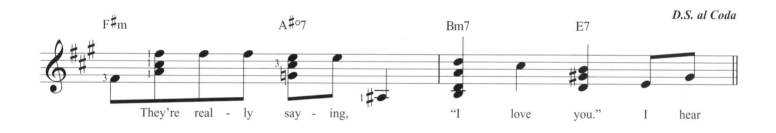

They're real - ly say - ing, "I love you." I hear

⊕ Coda

world! I think to my - self: ___

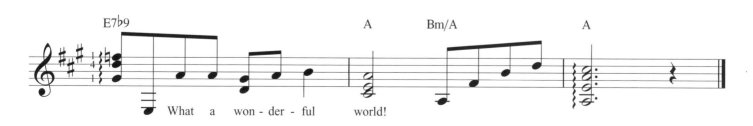

What a won - der - ful world!

You Are the Sunshine of My Life

Words and Music by Stevie Wonder

You are the sun-shine of ____ my life.

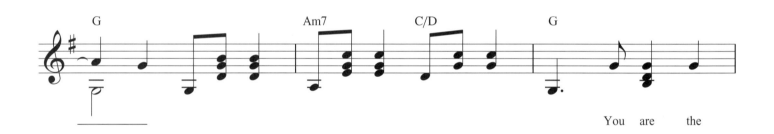

That's why I'll al - ways be ____ a - round. __

You are the

ap - ple of ____ my eye.

3rd time, to Coda

For - ev - er you'll stay in ____ my heart. ____

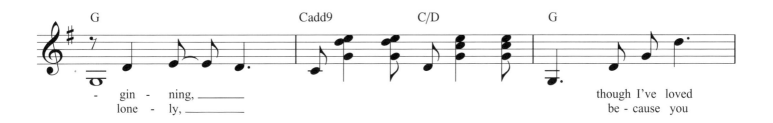

I feel like this is the be -
You must have known that I was

- gin - ning, _____
lone - ly, _____
though I've loved
be - cause you

you for a mil - lion years.
came to my res - cue.

And if I thought our love was end - ing, _____
And I know that this must be heav - en. _____

How I'd find my - self ___ drown - ing in my ___ own
How could so much love ___ be in - side ___ of

2nd time, D.C. al Coda

⊕ **Coda**

tears.
you?
Whoa, _____ whoa. ___
Whoa, _____ whoa. ___

The Entertainer

By Scott Joplin

Over the Rainbow

from THE WIZARD OF OZ

Music by Harold Arlen
Lyric by E.Y. "Yip" Harburg

Moderately

Some - where o - ver the rain - bow, way up
Some - where o - ver the rain - bow, skies are
Some - where o - ver the rain - bow, blue - birds

high, there's a land that I heard of
blue, and the dreams that you dare to
fly. Birds fly o - ver the rain - bow;

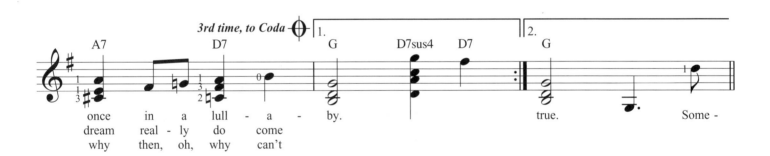

3rd time, to Coda

once in a lull - a - by. true. Some -
dream real - ly do come
why then, oh, why can't

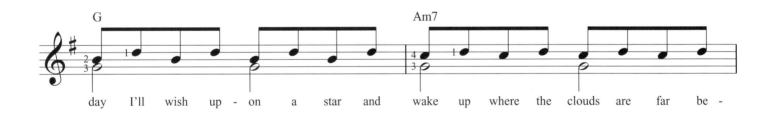

day I'll wish up - on a star and wake up where the clouds are far be -

hind me. Where trou - bles melt like lem - on drops, a -

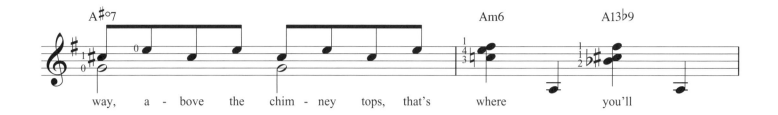

way, a - bove the chim - ney tops, that's where you'll

D.C. al Coda   ⊕ **Coda**

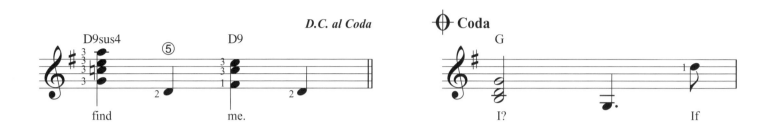

find me.   I?   If

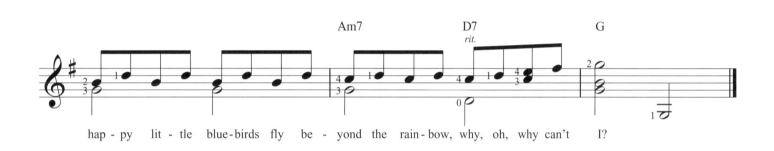

hap - py lit - tle blue-birds fly be - yond the rain - bow, why, oh, why can't I?

Time in a Bottle

Words and Music by Jim Croce

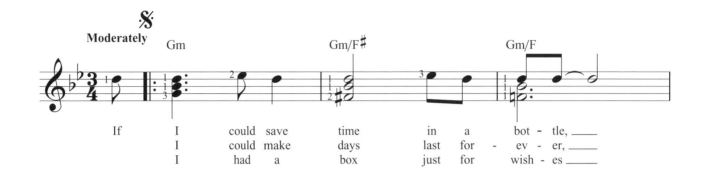

If I could save time in a bottle,
I could make days last for ev-er,
I had a box just for wish-es

the first thing that I'd like to do
if words could make wish-es come true,
and dreams that had nev-er come true,

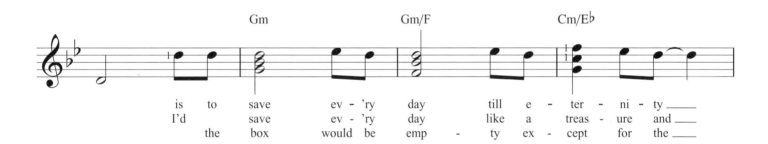

is to save ev-'ry day till e-ter-ni-ty
I'd save ev-'ry day like a treas-ure and
the box would be emp-ty ex-cept for the

pass-es a-way just to spend them with you.
then a-gain I would spend them with you. }
mem-'ry of how they were an-swered by you. }

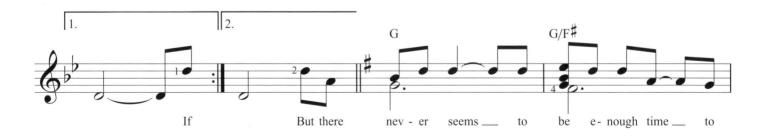

If But there nev-er seems to be e-nough time to

do   the   things ___ you   want   to   do   once   you   find   them.

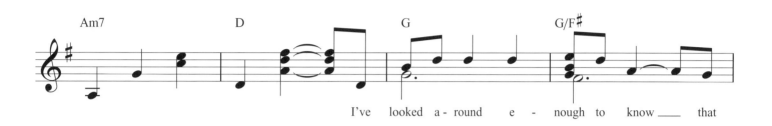

I've   looked   a - round   e - nough   to   know ___ that

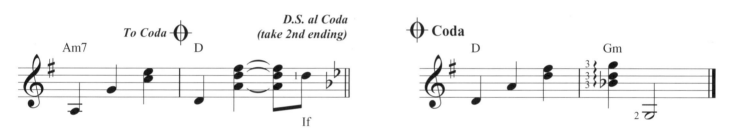

you're   the   one   I   want   to   go   through   time   with.

To Coda $\oplus$ ***D.S. al Coda***
(take 2nd ending) $\oplus$ **Coda**

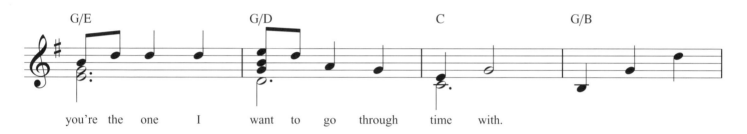

If

Beyond the Sea

Lyrics by Jack Lawrence
Music by Charles Trenet and Albert Lasry
Original French Lyric to "La Mer" by Charles Trenet

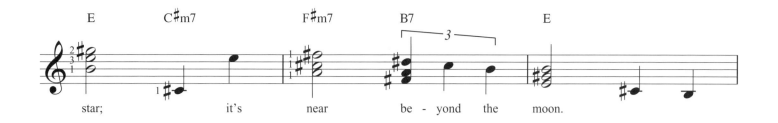

star; it's near be - yond the moon.

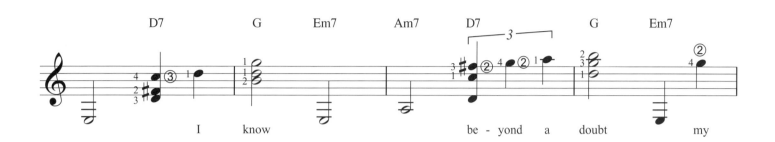

I know be - yond a doubt my

D.S. al Fine
(take 2nd ending)

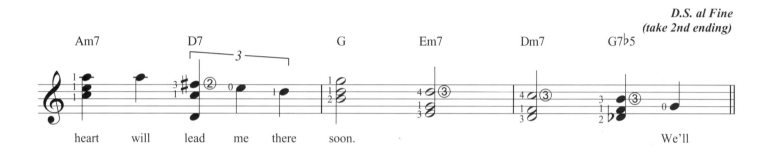

heart will lead me there soon. We'll

Goldfinger

Music by John Barry
Lyrics by Leslie Bricusse and Anthony Newley

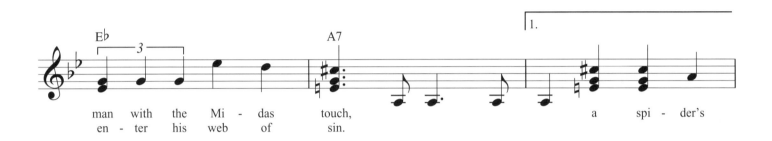

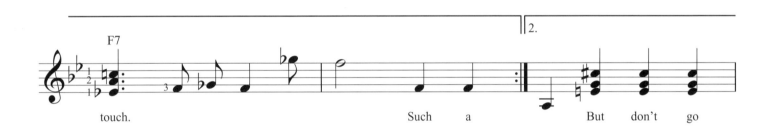

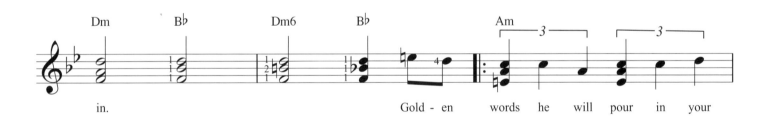

gold - en girl ___ knows when he's kissed her, it's the kiss of

death from Mis - ter Gold - fin - ger.

Pret - ty girl, be - ware of his heart of gold;

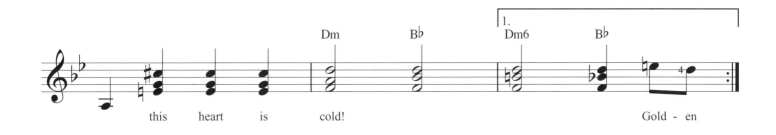

this heart is cold! Gold - en

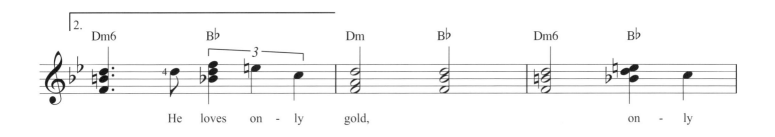

He loves on - ly gold, on - ly

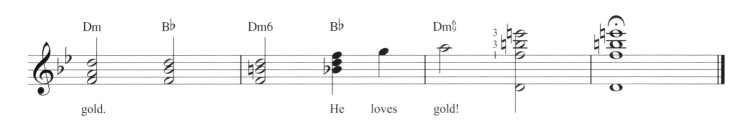

gold. He loves gold!

Hey Jude

Words and Music by John Lennon and Paul McCartney

I Will Survive

Words and Music by Dino Fekaris and Frederick J. Perren

Imagine

Words and Music by John Lennon

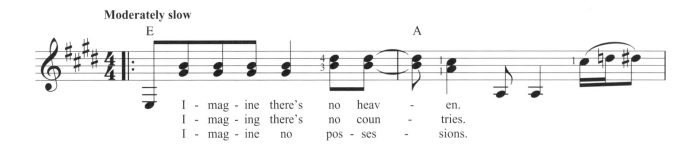

Moderately slow

I - mag - ine there's no heav - en.
I - mag - ing there's no coun - tries.
I - mag - ine no pos - ses - sions.

It's eas - y if you try. _____
It is - n't hard to do. _____
I won - der if you can. _____

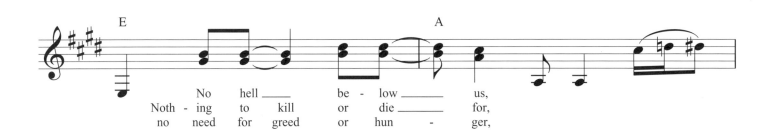

No hell _____ be - low _____ us,
Noth - ing to kill or die _____ for,
no need for greed or hun - ger,

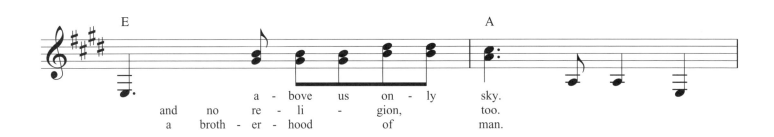

a - bove us on - ly sky.
and no re - li - gion, too.
a broth - er - hood of man.

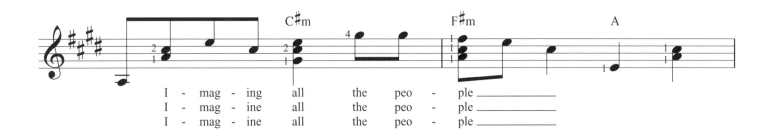

I - mag - ing all the peo - ple _____
I - mag - ine all the peo - ple _____
I - mag - ine all the peo - ple _____

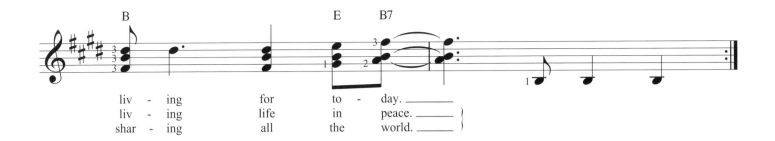

liv - ing for to - day. _____
liv - ing life in peace. _____
shar - ing all the world. _____

You may say _____ I'm a dream - er,

but I'm not the on - ly one.

To Coda ⊕

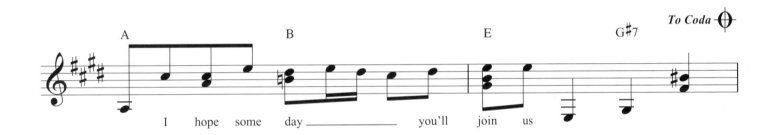

I hope some day _____ you'll join us

D.C. al Coda
(no repeat)

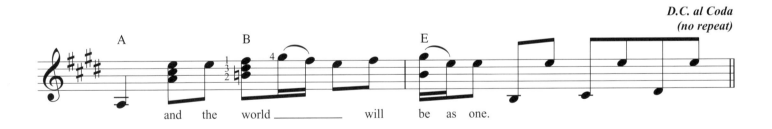

and the world _____ will be as one.

⊕ **Coda**

and the world _____ will live as one.

Don't Know Why

Words and Music by Jesse Harris

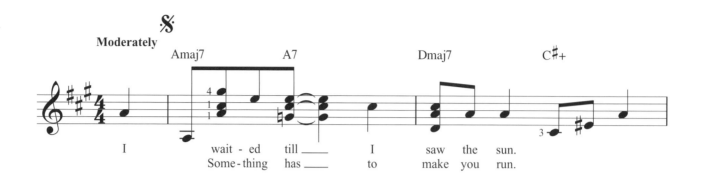

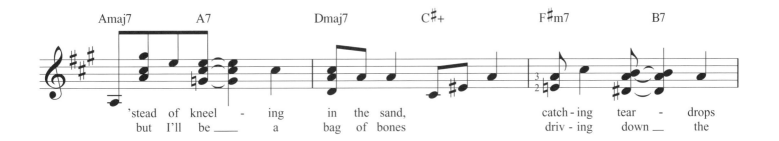

'stead of kneel - ing   in the sand,   catch - ing   tear - drops
but I'll be ___   a   bag of bones   driv - ing   down ___   the

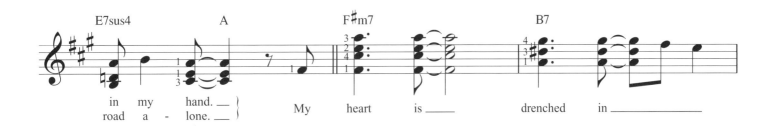

in   my   hand.   My   heart   is ___   drenched   in ___
road   a - lone. ___

wine,   but   you'll   be ___

2nd time, D.S. al Fine

on   my ___   mind   for - ev - er. ___

Fly Me to the Moon
(In Other Words)

Words and Music by Bart Howard

You've Got a Friend

Words and Music by Carole King

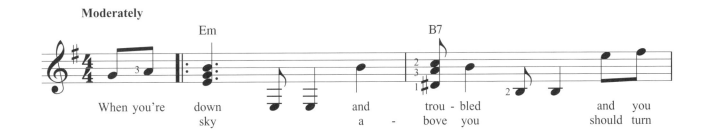

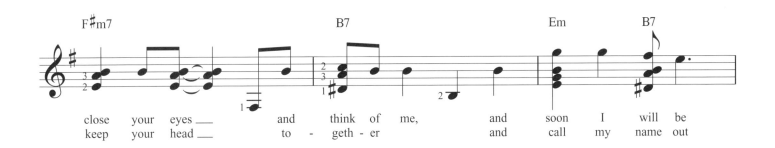

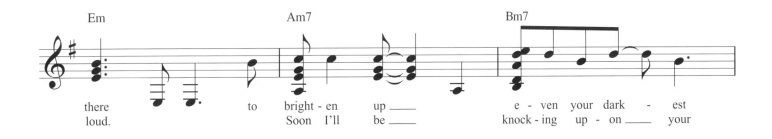

night.
door.

You just call out my

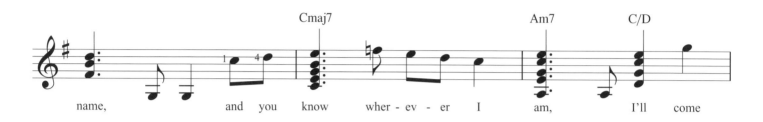

name, and you know wher-ev-er I am, I'll come

run-ning to see you a-gain.

Win-ter, spring, sum-mer or fall,_____

3rd time, to Coda

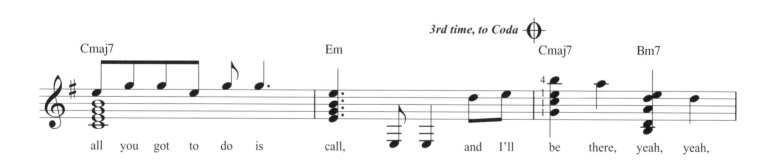

all you got to do is call, and I'll be there, yeah, yeah,

yeah. You've got a friend.

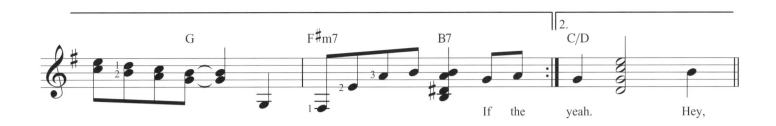

ain't it good to know that you've got a friend when peo-ple can be _____ so

cold? They'll hurt you and de - sert you. They'll

take you soul _____ if you let them. Yeah, but don't you let _____ them.

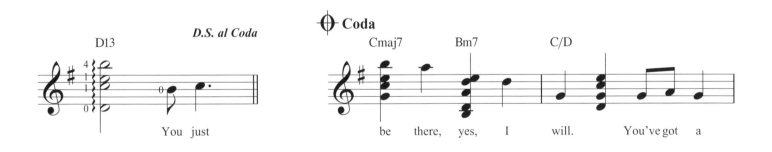

D.S. al Coda   ⊕ **Coda**

You just   be there, yes, I will.   You've got a

friend.

JAZZ GUITAR CHORD MELODY SOLOS

This series features chord melody arrangements in standard notation and tablature of songs for intermediate guitarists.

ALL-TIME STANDARDS INCLUDES TAB
27 songs, including: All of Me • Bewitched • Come Fly with Me • A Fine Romance • Georgia on My Mind • How High the Moon • I'll Never Smile Again • I've Got You Under My Skin • It's De-Lovely • It's Only a Paper Moon • My Romance • Satin Doll • The Surrey with the Fringe on Top • Yesterdays • and more.
00699757 Solo Guitar $14.99

CHRISTMAS CAROLS INCLUDES TAB
26 songs, including: Auld Lang Syne • Away in a Manger • Deck the Hall • God Rest Ye Merry, Gentlemen • Good King Wenceslas • Here We Come A-Wassailing • It Came upon the Midnight Clear • Joy to the World • O Holy Night • O Little Town of Bethlehem • Silent Night • Toyland • We Three Kings of Orient Are • and more.
00701697 Solo Guitar $12.99

DISNEY SONGS INCLUDES TAB
27 songs, including: Beauty and the Beast • Can You Feel the Love Tonight • Candle on the Water • Colors of the Wind • A Dream Is a Wish Your Heart Makes • Heigh-Ho • Some Day My Prince Will Come • Under the Sea • When You Wish upon a Star • A Whole New World (Aladdin's Theme) • Zip-A-Dee-Doo-Dah • and more.
00701902 Solo Guitar $14.99

DUKE ELLINGTON INCLUDES TAB
25 songs, including: C-Jam Blues • Caravan • Do Nothin' Till You Hear from Me • Don't Get Around Much Anymore • I Got It Bad and That Ain't Good • I'm Just a Lucky So and So • In a Sentimental Mood • It Don't Mean a Thing (If It Ain't Got That Swing) • Mood Indigo • Perdido • Prelude to a Kiss • Satin Doll • and more.
00700636 Solo Guitar $12.99

FAVORITE STANDARDS INCLUDES TAB
27 songs, including: All the Way • Autumn in New York • Blue Skies • Cheek to Cheek • Don't Get Around Much Anymore • How Deep Is the Ocean • I'll Be Seeing You • Isn't It Romantic? • It Could Happen to You • The Lady Is a Tramp • Moon River • Speak Low • Take the "A" Train • Willow Weep for Me • Witchcraft • and more.
00699756 Solo Guitar $14.99

FINGERPICKING JAZZ STANDARDS INCLUDES TAB
15 songs: Autumn in New York • Body and Soul • Can't Help Lovin' Dat Man • Easy Living • A Fine Romance • Have You Met Miss Jones? • I'm Beginning to See the Light • It Could Happen to You • My Romance • Stella by Starlight • Tangerine • The Very Thought of You • The Way You Look Tonight • When Sunny Gets Blue • Yesterdays.
00699840 Solo Guitar $7.99

JAZZ BALLADS INCLUDES TAB
27 songs, including: Body and Soul • Darn That Dream • Easy to Love (You'd Be So Easy to Love) • Here's That Rainy Day • In a Sentimental Mood • Misty • My Foolish Heart • My Funny Valentine • The Nearness of You • Stella by Starlight • Time After Time • The Way You Look Tonight • When Sunny Gets Blue • and more.
00699755 Solo Guitar $14.99

JAZZ CLASSICS INCLUDES TAB
27 songs, including: Blue in Green • Bluesette • Bouncing with Bud • Cast Your Fate to the Wind • Con Alma • Doxy • Epistrophy • Footprints • Giant Steps • Invitation • Lullaby of Birdland • Lush Life • A Night in Tunisia • Nuages • Ruby, My Dear • St. Thomas • Stolen Moments • Waltz for Debby • Yardbird Suite • and more.
00699758 Solo Guitar $14.99

Prices, content, and availability subject to change without notice. | Disney characters and artwork ©Disney Enterprises, Inc.

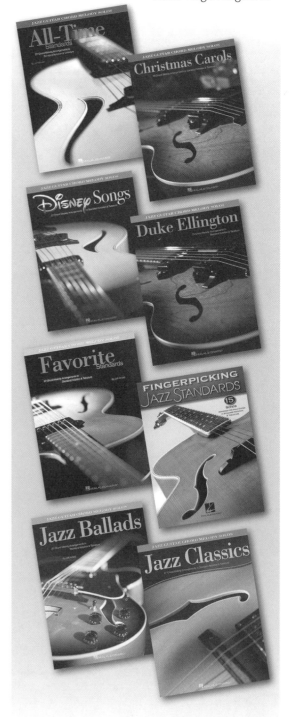

HAL•LEONARD®
www.halleonard.com

AUTHENTIC CHORDS • ORIGINAL KEYS • COMPLETE SONGS

The *Strum It* series lets players strum the chords and sing along with their favorite hits. Each song has been selected because it can be played with regular open chords, barre chords, or other moveable chord types. Guitarists can simply play the rhythm, or play and sing along through the entire song. All songs are shown in their original keys complete with chords, strum patterns, melody and lyrics. Wherever possible, the chord voicings from the recorded versions are notated.

THE BEACH BOYS' GREATEST HITS
_____00699357.............................$12.95

THE BEATLES FAVORITES
_____00699249.............................$14.95

BEST OF CONTEMPORARY CHRISTIAN
_____00699531.............................$12.95

VERY BEST OF JOHNNY CASH
_____00699514.............................$14.99

CELTIC GUITAR SONGBOOK
_____00699265...............................$9.95

CHRISTMAS SONGS FOR GUITAR
_____00699247.............................$10.95

CHRISTMAS SONGS WITH 3 CHORDS
_____00699487...............................$8.95

VERY BEST OF ERIC CLAPTON
_____00699560.............................$12.95

COUNTRY STRUMMIN'
_____00699119...............................$8.95

JIM CROCE – CLASSIC HITS
_____00699269.............................$10.95

VERY BEST OF JOHN DENVER
_____00699488.............................$12.95

NEIL DIAMOND
_____00699593.............................$12.95

DISNEY FAVORITES
_____00699171.............................$10.95

MELISSA ETHERIDGE GREATEST HITS
_____00699518.............................$12.99

FAVORITE SONGS WITH 3 CHORDS
_____00699112...............................$8.95

FAVORITE SONGS WITH 4 CHORDS
_____00699270...............................$8.95

FIRESIDE SING-ALONG
_____00699273...............................$8.95

FOLK FAVORITES
_____00699517...............................$8.95

THE GUITAR STRUMMERS' ROCK SONGBOOK
_____00701678.............................$14.99

BEST OF WOODY GUTHRIE
_____00699496.............................$12.95

JOHN HIATT COLLECTION
_____00699398.............................$12.95

THE VERY BEST OF BOB MARLEY
_____00699524.............................$12.95

A MERRY CHRISTMAS SONGBOOK
_____00699211...............................$9.95

MORE FAVORITE SONGS WITH 3 CHORDS
_____00699532...............................$8.95

THE VERY BEST OF TOM PETTY
_____00699336.............................$12.95

POP-ROCK GUITAR FAVORITES
_____00699088...............................$8.95

ELVIS! GREATEST HITS
_____00699276.............................$10.95

BEST OF GEORGE STRAIT
_____00699235.............................$14.99

TAYLOR SWIFT FOR ACOUSTIC GUITAR
_____00109717.............................$16.99

BEST OF HANK WILLIAMS JR.
_____00699224.............................$14.99

HAL•LEONARD®

7777 W. BLUEMOUND RD. P.O. BOX 13819
MILWAUKEE, WISCONSIN 53213

Visit Hal Leonard online at **www.halleonard.com**

Prices, contents & availability subject to change without notice.

0215

This series will help you play your favorite songs quickly and easily. Just follow the tab and listen to the audio to the hear how the guitar should sound, and then play along using the separate backing tracks. Mac or PC users can also slow down the tempo without changing pitch by using the CD in their computer. The melody and lyrics are included in the book so that you can sing or simply follow along.

INCLUDES TAB

VOL. 1 – ROCK	00699570 / $16.99	
VOL. 2 – ACOUSTIC	00699569 / $16.95	
VOL. 3 – HARD ROCK	00699573 / $16.95	
VOL. 4 – POP/ROCK	00699571 / $16.99	
VOL. 5 – MODERN ROCK	00699574 / $16.99	
VOL. 6 – '90S ROCK	00699572 / $16.99	
VOL. 7 – BLUES	00699575 / $16.95	
VOL. 8 – ROCK	00699585 / $14.99	
VOL. 10 – ACOUSTIC	00699586 / $16.95	
VOL. 11 – EARLY ROCK	00699579 / $14.95	
VOL. 12 – POP/ROCK	00699587 / $14.95	
VOL. 13 – FOLK ROCK	00699581 / $15.99	
VOL. 14 – BLUES ROCK	00699582 / $16.95	
VOL. 15 – R&B	00699583 / $14.95	
VOL. 16 – JAZZ	00699584 / $15.95	
VOL. 17 – COUNTRY	00699588 / $15.95	
VOL. 18 – ACOUSTIC ROCK	00699577 / $15.95	
VOL. 19 – SOUL	00699578 / $14.99	
VOL. 20 – ROCKABILLY	00699580 / $14.95	
VOL. 21 – YULETIDE	00699602 / $14.95	
VOL. 22 – CHRISTMAS	00699600 / $15.95	
VOL. 23 – SURF	00699635 / $14.95	
VOL. 24 – ERIC CLAPTON	00699649 / $17.99	
VOL. 25 – LENNON & MCCARTNEY	00699642 / $16.99	
VOL. 26 – ELVIS PRESLEY	00699643 / $14.95	
VOL. 27 – DAVID LEE ROTH	00699645 / $16.95	
VOL. 28 – GREG KOCH	00699646 / $14.95	
VOL. 29 – BOB SEGER	00699647 / $15.99	
VOL. 30 – KISS	00699644 / $16.99	
VOL. 31 – CHRISTMAS HITS	00699652 / $14.95	
VOL. 32 – THE OFFSPRING	00699653 / $14.95	
VOL. 33 – ACOUSTIC CLASSICS	00699656 / $16.95	
VOL. 34 – CLASSIC ROCK	00699658 / $16.95	
VOL. 35 – HAIR METAL	00699660 / $16.95	
VOL. 36 – SOUTHERN ROCK	00699661 / $16.95	
VOL. 37 – ACOUSTIC UNPLUGGED	00699662 / $22.99	
VOL. 38 – BLUES	00699663 / $16.95	
VOL. 39 – '80S METAL	00699664 / $16.99	
VOL. 40 – INCUBUS	00699668 / $17.95	
VOL. 41 – ERIC CLAPTON	00699669 / $16.95	
VOL. 42 – 2000S ROCK	00699670 / $16.99	
VOL. 43 – LYNYRD SKYNYRD	00699681 / $17.95	
VOL. 44 – JAZZ	00699689 / $14.99	
VOL. 45 – TV THEMES	00699718 / $14.95	
VOL. 46 – MAINSTREAM ROCK	00699722 / $16.95	
VOL. 47 – HENDRIX SMASH HITS	00699723 / $19.95	
VOL. 48 – AEROSMITH CLASSICS	00699724 / $17.99	
VOL. 49 – STEVIE RAY VAUGHAN	00699725 / $17.99	
VOL. 50 – VAN HALEN 1978-1984	00110269 / $17.99	
VOL. 51 – ALTERNATIVE '90S	00699727 / $14.99	
VOL. 52 – FUNK	00699728 / $14.95	
VOL. 53 – DISCO	00699729 / $14.99	
VOL. 54 – HEAVY METAL	00699730 / $14.95	
VOL. 55 – POP METAL	00699731 / $14.95	
VOL. 56 – FOO FIGHTERS	00699749 / $15.99	
VOL. 57 – SYSTEM OF A DOWN	00699751 / $14.95	
VOL. 58 – BLINK-182	00699772 / $14.95	
VOL. 59 – CHET ATKINS	00702347 / $16.99	
VOL. 60 – 3 DOORS DOWN	00699774 / $14.95	
VOL. 61 – SLIPKNOT	00699775 / $16.99	
VOL. 62 – CHRISTMAS CAROLS	00699798 / $12.95	

VOL. 63 – CREEDENCE CLEARWATER REVIVAL	00699802 / $16.99	
VOL. 64 – THE ULTIMATE OZZY OSBOURNE	00699803 / $16.99	
VOL. 66 – THE ROLLING STONES	00699807 / $16.95	
VOL. 67 – BLACK SABBATH	00699808 / $16.99	
VOL. 68 – PINK FLOYD – DARK SIDE OF THE MOON	00699809 / $16.99	
VOL. 69 – ACOUSTIC FAVORITES	00699810 / $14.95	
VOL. 70 – OZZY OSBOURNE	00699805 / $16.99	
VOL. 71 – CHRISTIAN ROCK	00699824 / $14.95	
VOL. 73 – BLUESY ROCK	00699829 / $16.99	
VOL. 75 – TOM PETTY	00699882 / $16.99	
VOL. 76 – COUNTRY HITS	00699884 / $14.95	
VOL. 77 – BLUEGRASS	00699910 / $14.99	
VOL. 78 – NIRVANA	00700132 / $16.99	
VOL. 79 – NEIL YOUNG	00700133 / $24.99	
VOL. 80 – ACOUSTIC ANTHOLOGY	00700175 / $19.95	
VOL. 81 – ROCK ANTHOLOGY	00700176 / $22.99	
VOL. 82 – EASY SONGS	00700177 / $12.99	
VOL. 83 – THREE CHORD SONGS	00700178 / $16.99	
VOL. 84 – STEELY DAN	00700200 / $16.99	
VOL. 85 – THE POLICE	00700269 / $16.99	
VOL. 86 – BOSTON	00700465 / $16.99	
VOL. 87 – ACOUSTIC WOMEN	00700763 / $14.99	
VOL. 88 – GRUNGE	00700467 / $16.99	
VOL. 89 – REGGAE	00700468 / $15.99	
VOL. 90 – CLASSICAL POP	00700469 / $14.99	
VOL. 91 – BLUES INSTRUMENTALS	00700505 / $14.99	
VOL. 92 – EARLY ROCK INSTRUMENTALS	00700506 / $14.99	
VOL. 93 – ROCK INSTRUMENTALS	00700507 / $16.99	
VOL. 94 – SLOW BLUES	00700508 / $16.99	
VOL. 95 – BLUES CLASSICS	00700509 / $14.99	
VOL. 96 – THIRD DAY	00700560 / $14.95	
VOL. 97 – ROCK BAND	00700703 / $14.99	
VOL. 99 – ZZ TOP	00700762 / $16.99	
VOL. 100 – B.B. KING	00700466 / $16.99	
VOL. 101 – SONGS FOR BEGINNERS	00701917 / $14.99	
VOL. 102 – CLASSIC PUNK	00700769 / $14.99	
VOL. 103 – SWITCHFOOT	00700773 / $16.99	
VOL. 104 – DUANE ALLMAN	00700846 / $16.99	
VOL. 105 – LATIN	00700939 / $16.99	
VOL. 106 – WEEZER	00700958 / $14.99	
VOL. 107 – CREAM	00701069 / $16.99	
VOL. 108 – THE WHO	00701053 / $16.99	
VOL. 109 – STEVE MILLER	00701054 / $14.99	
VOL. 110 – SLIDE GUITAR HITS	00701055 / $16.99	
VOL. 111 – JOHN MELLENCAMP	00701056 / $14.99	
VOL. 112 – QUEEN	00701052 / $16.99	
VOL. 113 – JIM CROCE	00701058 / $15.99	
VOL. 114 – BON JOVI	00701060 / $14.99	
VOL. 115 – JOHNNY CASH	00701070 / $16.99	
VOL. 116 – THE VENTURES	00701124 / $14.99	
VOL. 117 – BRAD PAISLEY	00701224 / $16.99	
VOL. 118 – ERIC JOHNSON	00701353 / $16.99	
VOL. 119 – AC/DC CLASSICS	00701356 / $17.99	
VOL. 120 – PROGRESSIVE ROCK	00701457 / $14.99	
VOL. 121 – U2	00701508 / $16.99	
VOL. 122 – CROSBY, STILLS & NASH	00701610 / $16.99	
VOL. 123 – LENNON & MCCARTNEY ACOUSTIC	00701614 / $16.99	
VOL. 125 – JEFF BECK	00701687 / $16.99	

VOL. 126 – BOB MARLEY	00701701 / $16.99	
VOL. 127 – 1970S ROCK	00701739 / $14.99	
VOL. 128 – 1960S ROCK	00701740 / $14.99	
VOL. 129 – MEGADETH	00701741 / $16.99	
VOL. 131 – 1990S ROCK	00701743 / $14.99	
VOL. 132 – COUNTRY ROCK	00701757 / $15.99	
VOL. 133 – TAYLOR SWIFT	00701894 / $16.99	
VOL. 134 – AVENGED SEVENFOLD	00701906 / $16.99	
VOL. 136 – GUITAR THEMES	00701922 / $14.99	
VOL. 137 – IRISH TUNES	00701966 / $15.99	
VOL. 138 – BLUEGRASS CLASSICS	00701967 / $14.99	
VOL. 139 – GARY MOORE	00702370 / $16.99	
VOL. 140 – MORE STEVIE RAY VAUGHAN	00702396 / $17.99	
VOL. 141 – ACOUSTIC HITS	00702401 / $16.99	
VOL. 143 – SLASH	00702425 / $19.99	
VOL. 144 – DJANGO REINHARDT	00702531 / $16.99	
VOL. 145 – DEF LEPPARD	00702532 / $16.99	
VOL. 146 – ROBERT JOHNSON	00702533 / $16.99	
VOL. 147 – SIMON & GARFUNKEL	14041591 / $16.99	
VOL. 148 – BOB DYLAN	14041592 / $16.99	
VOL. 149 – AC/DC HITS	14041593 / $17.99	
VOL. 150 – ZAKK WYLDE	02501717 / $16.99	
VOL. 152 – JOE BONAMASSA	02501751 / $19.99	
VOL. 153 – RED HOT CHILI PEPPERS	00702990 / $19.99	
VOL. 155 – ERIC CLAPTON – FROM THE ALBUM UNPLUGGED	00703085 / $16.99	
VOL. 156 – SLAYER	00703770 / $17.99	
VOL. 157 – FLEETWOOD MAC	00101382 / $16.99	
VOL. 158 – ULTIMATE CHRISTMAS	00101889 / $14.99	
VOL. 159 – WES MONTGOMERY	00102593 / $19.99	
VOL. 160 – T-BONE WALKER	00102641 / $16.99	
VOL. 161 – THE EAGLES – ACOUSTIC	00102659 / $17.99	
VOL. 162 – THE EAGLES HITS	00102667 / $17.99	
VOL. 163 – PANTERA	00103036 / $17.99	
VOL. 164 – VAN HALEN 1986-1995	00110270 / $17.99	
VOL. 166 – MODERN BLUES	00700764 / $16.99	
VOL. 168 – KISS	00113421 / $16.99	
VOL. 169 – TAYLOR SWIFT	00115982 / $16.99	
VOL. 170 – THREE DAYS GRACE	00117337 / $16.99	
VOL. 171 – JAMES BROWN	00117420 / $16.99	
VOL. 172 – THE DOOBIE BROTHERS	00119670 / $16.99	
VOL. 174 – SCORPIONS	00122119 / $16.99	
VOL. 175 – MICHAEL SCHENKER	00122127 / $16.99	
VOL. 176 – BLUES BREAKERS WITH JOHN MAYALL & ERIC CLAPTON	00122132 / $19.99	
VOL. 177 – ALBERT KING	00123271 / $16.99	
VOL. 178 – JASON MRAZ	00124165 / $17.99	
VOL. 179 – RAMONES	00127073 / $16.99	
VOL. 180 – BRUNO MARS	00129706 / $16.99	
VOL. 181 – JACK JOHNSON	00129854 / $16.99	
VOL. 182 – SOUNDGARDEN	00138161 / $17.99	
VOL. 184 – KENNY WAYNE SHEPHERD	00138258 / $17.99	
VOL. 187 – JOHN DENVER	00140839 / $17.99	

Complete song lists available online.

Prices, contents, and availability subject to change without notice.

HAL•LEONARD® CORPORATION

7777 W. BLUEMOUND RD. P.O. BOX 13819 Milwaukee, WI 53213

www.halleonard.com

1215